Beowulf

The New Translation

Gerald J. Davis

Insignia Publishing

Translation copyright 2013 by Gerald J. Davis

ISBN 978-1491250181
(Paperback)

Insignia Publishing

Bridgeport, Connecticut

Beowulf

Beowulf   2

For Peter and Jennifer

...

Also by Gerald J. Davis

Don Quixote, The New Translation

Left No Forwarding Address

Jungle of Glass

A Murder Too Personal

...

Contents

...

Beowulf   10

A Note on the Translation

By

Gerald J. Davis

    J. R. R. Tolkien, in his famous 1936 lecture, *Beowulf: The Monsters and the Critics,* said of *Beowulf,* "It is a work of genius, rare and surprising in the period, and it is worth studying. (*Beowulf*) is a poem by an Englishman using, afresh, ancient and largely traditional material. The high tone, the sense of dignity, alone, is evidence in *Beowulf* of the presence of a mind lofty and thoughtful. In *Beowulf* we have an historical poem about the pagan past. It is a poem by a learned man writing of old times who, looking back on the heroism and sorrow, feels in them something permanent and something symbolical...

    "*Beowulf* is not an actual picture of historic Denmark or Geatland or Sweden about A.D. 500. But it is, on a general view, a self-consistent picture, a construction bearing clearly the marks of design and thought. The whole must have succeeded admirably in creating, in the minds of the poet's contemporaries, the illusion of surveying a past, pagan but noble, and fraught with a deep significance—a past that itself had depth and reached backward into a dark antiquity of sorrow.

    "We may be thankful that the product of so noble a temper has been preserved by chance (if such it be) from the dragon of destruction."

    [Here Tolkien is referring to the Cotton Library fire in 1731 which burned parts of some edges of the only extant copy of the *Beowulf* manuscript.]

    "*Beowulf* is, indeed, the most successful Old English poem because, in it, the elements of language, metre, theme, structure are all most nearly in harmony.

    "If the funeral of Beowulf moved once like the echo of an ancient dirge, far-off and hopeless, it is to us as a memory brought over the hills, an echo of an echo...It is written in a language that, after many centuries, still has essential kinship with our own. It was made in this land, and moves in our northern world beneath our northern sky, and for those who are native to that tongue and land, it must ever call with a profound appeal—until the dragon comes."

Tolkien devoted a major part of his academic life at Oxford to the study of *Beowulf* and, almost singlehandedly, through his efforts, brought this oldest and longest Anglo-Saxon epic poem to the public's attention after centuries of neglect. Tolkien, indeed, wrote a translation of and commentary on *Beowulf*, which remain, unpublished, to this day, among the archives of the Bodleian Library at Oxford. It is certain that this epic served as a significant inspiration for Tolkien's later works, such as *The Hobbit* and *The Lord of the Rings*.

The origins, history and authorship of *Beowulf* are shrouded in uncertainty. It is fairly clear that the events depicted in the story take place during the late fifth to early sixth century A.D., because there is historical evidence that King Hygelac of the Geats was killed in a battle in France between the Geats and the Franks about 516-521 A.D. Certain other personages named in the poem, such as Ohthere, Eadgils and Ongentheow have been proven to be real historical figures and we can date them with some degree of confidence.

This heroic epic probably began, as most do, with a wandering troubadour strumming a stringed instrument, sitting before a hearth-fire, and singing the verses to a spellbound audience arrayed before him. At some point, the words of the troubadour were written down in a manuscript form, in order to preserve the story for posterity. There is great dispute among scholars as to when the manuscript itself was actually transcribed. Tolkien believed it was written about the eighth century, while other serious experts assert it was written as late as the early eleventh century.

As stated earlier, there is only one manuscript of *Beowulf* in existence. It is known as the Nowell Codex and is to be found in the British Library. The manuscript was evidently written by two distinct scribes, because the first 1939 lines are written in one handwriting and the remaining 1243 are written in another. Both scribes took meticulous care in transcribing the material, and their painstaking efforts are immediately evident to the diligent observer. However the provenance and subsequent ownership of the manuscript are unknown until it appeared in the library of Laurence Nowell (1515-1571), a tutor to Edward de Vere, 17th Earl of Oxford (1550-1604). The manuscript then made its way to the library of Robert Bruce Cotton, 1st Baronet of Connington (1570-1631), where it was damaged by a fire in 1731, when the edges of the manuscript were singed and the pages shriveled. The *Beowulf* manuscript, together with the rest of the impressive collection of the Cotton Library, was donated by a descendant of Robert Bruce Cotton,

Sir John Cotton, to the nation of England, and it is now housed in the British Library, where it is designated as Cotton Vitellius A.xv. The first actual reference to the manuscript appeared between 1628 and 1650 and was written by Franciscus Junius, the Younger (1591-1677), a collector of old manuscripts.

Subsequently, there appeared two catalogs of the contents of the Cotton Library. The first, in 1696, was assembled by the Reverend Thomas Smith (1638-1710), who was in charge of the Library for twelve years. The second was compiled by Humfrey Wanley (1672-1726), and the first official recorded notice of the manuscript appeared in his 1705 Catalog of Anglo-Saxon Manuscripts.

Portions of *Beowulf* were first published in English in 1805 by the historian Sharon Turner (1768-1847), and he deserves full credit for bringing to the attention of the English people the importance of this heroic elegy.

The first complete translation of *Beowulf* was written by Grimur Jonsson Thorkelin (1752-1829), an Icelandic scholar employed by the Danish civil service, and was published in 1815. Thorkelin's translation was written in Latin and it contained numerous textual errors which were uncovered by experts in later years.

An early translation of *Beowulf* which received high praise from academics was the 1837 prose version written by John Mitchell Kemble (1807-1857). It was lauded for Kemble's extensive scholarship and for its faithfulness to the original. Another important and highly-regarded verse translation of *Beowulf* was published in 1892 by John Lesslie Hall (1856-1928).

The poetical device employed in *Beowulf* is not rhyme, but alliteration, the rhythmic repetition of initial sounds of the words. Each line is divided into two parts separated by a pause, called a caesura. There are four beats in each line; that is to say, two beats in each half-line.

These are the opening lines of *Beowulf*:

HWEAT WE GARDE-na   in gear dagum
theod cyninga   thrym ge-frunon
hu tha aethelingas   ellen fremedon.

This may be roughly translated as:

Hark! The Spear-Danes, in earlier days,
King of the people, power we have heard of,
how the Princes, deeds of valor accomplished.

Several other poetic devices are used in this work, such as kennings, which are compound-word metaphors like whale-road for the sea and heaven's candle for the sun, and this is common to many classic Old English poems.

This translation attempts to render the poetry of *Beowulf* in the form of prose. Alliteration is used to a considerable extent, and it is hoped that the reader will read the story aloud, in order to hear the rhythmic cadences of the words. In doing so, one may thereby recall the pounding sonorities of Kipling and Pindar.

Beowulf is a pagan story overlaid with a patina of Christianity. The setting is a pre-Christian world which was just beginning to listen to the sermons of itinerant Christian preachers. It may be that the scribes who copied out the manuscript were Christian monks who sought to bring the blessings of Christ to these benighted heathens who populated the retelling of this "heroic elegy," as Tolkien termed it. Perhaps, in their candle-lit monastery, they hunched over their manuscripts and scratched out additions and emendations to make it more acceptable to the members of their faith. We do not know, and will probably never know.

We will probably also never ascertain what befell the Geats after the age of Beowulf. That tribe seems to have disappeared from view and there is scant evidence or record of these people in subsequent historical documents. There is some conjecture that the Geats were defeated by, and became part of, the nation that is now Sweden.

This translation of *Beowulf* is based chiefly upon the works by Kemble and Hall. There are no footnotes or endnotes. The audience who listened to the minstrel's rendition of this epic did not need explanations to further their understanding of it. If any explanations or clarifications are required, they are embedded in the body of the text, so as not to interrupt the flow of the words. After all, as Noel Coward once famously remarked, "Having to read a footnote resembles having to go downstairs to answer the door while in the midst of making love."

Every translation is an interpretation and a series of acts of selection, judgment and calculation. Any mistakes or faults in this edition are solely those of the translator.

And so, herewith, is a rousing heroic adventure story that comes to us down through the dim mists of antiquity.

Black Rock
2013

Beowulf

Hearken unto this tale of the glory of the Spear-Danes, renowned for their splendid deeds in bygone days. These mighty kings made manifest their valor and nobility, and were famous for their prowess in battle. We have heard of the honor these heroic warriors won.

Oft did Shield Sheafson, beset by his enemies from many tribes, wage relentless warfare against them, thus terrifying his foes. This selfsame Shield was first found as a babe, friendless and wretched, a foundling. But then Fate favored him and saw to his ascent, for he grew powerful under the Heavens and gained veneration and wealth, until the people, both far and near, who lived upon the shores of the whale-road, were compelled to bow unto his bidding and render him tribute. He was a great king.

After, to Shield was born a son called Beo, whom Heaven had sent to solace the folk, for they had suffered over the space of so long a time when they lacked a leader. Whereupon, the Lord of Life, the Wielder of Glory, upon Beo bestowed the world's esteem.

Beo, the son of Shield, was famed throughout the Danish lands and far spread his repute among the nations.

It is wise of a young prince, while still under the shelter of his father, to lavish gifts and fees upon his father's friends, so that, when he comes of age and war draws nigh, loyal liegemen shall stand steadfastly by his side. Through praise-worthy actions will a nobleman gain laurels among all the clans.

At the hour that was appointed by Fate, Shield passed under the protection of God. His dear kinsmen bore him unto the shore of the oceans' swells, as he had besought them to do when he did long rule them as their well-loved prince.

There, in the current, rocked the ring-prowed ship, ice-covered, set to sail, a vessel fit for a chieftain. Then they laid their beloved leader, the mighty one, the generous giver of gifts, upon the widest part of the deck of the ship, beside the mast. Many a treasure and ornament, fetched from far lands, were placed near unto him. Never heard I of a more comely ship adorned with weapons of warfare and with war-weeds, with sword-blade and with breast-plate. Upon his bosom lay a heaped hoard of riches that, ere long, would float away with him, far o'er the flood. They festooned him with no less lordly treasure than those who, in former times, had sent him forth to sail alone upon the seas, a mere youngling. Then they unfurled a golden banner high over his head, outstretched under Heaven, and let the billows bear him seaward. Sad was their spirit and mournful was their mood. No man is able to tell us, no sage in a palace, no hero beneath Heaven, whither that craft drifted or who recovered that cargo.

I

Then Beo ruled for many years in the land of Shield's clan. He was a beloved sovereign, famous among the folk after his father had passed hence, the Prince from his earthly dwelling. Unto Beo an heir was born, noble Healfdene, who graciously governed the Danes over the course of his long life and proved unvanquished in combat. This warrior Prince begat four children, Heorogar, Hrothgar, Halga the Brave, and Yrse, who, I heard, was Queen and consort to Onela, King of the Swedes, and dearly-cherished bedmate of this war leader.

To Hrothgar was granted such success in battle and glory in combat that all his kin obeyed his bidding, and his band of youthful followers grew to be a mighty army.

Hrothgar then took it into his mind to command the people to construct a mighty building, a great mead-hall, which the sons of men would celebrate for ages to come. Therein would he allot, to young and old, all the spoils of battle which the Lord had bestowed upon him, save for common lands and the lives of slaves. Then heard I that, far and wide, orders were given unto many a tribe to build and adorn this great mead-hall. Quickly it came to pass that it was completed, as Hrothgar had ordered, the greatest of hall-buildings. He whose word held wide sway over many a land named it Heorot.

Whereupon, Hrothgar broke not his vow. He commanded a banquet to be held, and granted rings and riches to those who gathered at the table. The great hall towered over the countryside, tall and wide-gabled, awaiting the fierce flames of the raging fire that would, in time, engulf it, when the fatal feud between Hrothgar and his daughter's husband would burn Heorot to the ground.

Then a powerful demon, who dwelt in darkness, grew exceeding wrathful upon hearing the din of light-hearted revelry and the music of merry-making that issued forth from the mead-hall every day. There was dulcet harp music and the sweet song of the minstrel, singing of the creation of Man, of how the Almighty wrought the world, of fairest fields enfolded by water, of how He gloriously set the Sun and Moon to lavish their luster upon the land-dwellers, of how He adorned the face of the Earth with boughs and leaves, and of how life also He created for every creature that breathes and moves under Heaven.

Thus abided these noble warriors amidst pleasure and plenty, till a fiend from the Netherworld began to wreak Evil, that specialty of Hell. This dreadful demon was called Grendel. He haunted the moors, dwelt in the marshes, the desolate heaths and wasted swamps. This wretched creature had sojourned for a time in the land of the race of giants, that spawn of Cain, whom the Creator had exiled forever for the killing of Abel. The Almighty rejoiced not in that feud, but banished Cain far from the sight of mankind for that misdeed. From thence, sprang all manner of ill-favored creatures, ogres, evil spirits, goblins, sea-monsters, as well as the giants who strove against God for many eons, until He finally exacted fitting retribution upon them in the Great Flood.

II

Then, when night was come, Grendel went forth unto the great hall to see how the warriors betook themselves to rest after their reveling was done. And, therein, he found them, this band of noblemen, reposing after the feast, thinking not on sorrow or misfortune or the misery of man. Whereupon, Grendel tarried but little. This monster of damnation, grim and greedy, savage and strong, seized thirty thanes from their slumbers and slew them. From thence he hastened unto his lair, laden with the carcasses of the slaughtered, exulting in his prey.

In the light of dawn, as the day was breaking, the men came to know the fearsome might of Grendel. Then was a great lamentation upraised after the feasting, a heartfelt cry of mourning. Hrothgar, the renowned ruler, a leader exceeding good, sat stricken and sorrowful. When he saw the tracks of that hateful fiend, that accursed demon, Hrothgar suffered bitterly and sorrowed for his lost men. His distress was too hard, too long and too unbearable.

It was not a longer lapse than the next night when Grendel began anew his ruthless rampage. The monster felt no remorse, for he was too bent on malice and murder. Wherefore, the warriors sought out a safer distance and slept at night in the outbuildings, a bed after the banquet, when they saw manifest the hatred of that hall-haunting demon. Those who did outrun the fiend fled far and fast.

Thus Grendel ruled unrighteous and raged against all, until empty and deserted stood that best of lordly buildings. Long was the season of woe. For the space of twelve winters, Hrothgar, King of the Danes, suffered every affliction and every sadness. Wherefore, it came to be well known among the children of men, in sorrowful songs, that Grendel waged long war against Hrothgar, and maintained his murderous malice, an unflagging feud and bitter enmity. They sang that the monster wished no peace with any man of the Danish race, and would not lay aside his blood lust, nor consent to settle for gold. Neither did any counselor expect to receive fair reparation from the hands of this foul fiend.

The monster, dark as the shadow of death, ambushed both young and old and dogged them over mist-covered moorlands, lurking there in the long hours of the night, for men know not where the haunts of these creatures from Hell may be.

So the foe of mankind continued his crimes, coming alone in the darkness to inflict grievous injuries upon the people. Grendel dwelt in Heorot at night, that treasure-bedecked hall, but never dared to sit upon the precious throne of King Hrothgar, for fear of the Almighty. This was because the Lord's love Grendel knew not.

That was a time of soul-crushing sorrow and misery for Hrothgar. He sat often in council with his ministers, seeking advice as to what was best for strong-hearted men to do against the dread of sudden onslaughts. And, sometimes, in desperation, they worshiped the old pagan idols and made heathen vows, praying that the Devil from Hell should succor them and ease the people's pain. Such was their way and their heathen hope, for their thoughts turned toward Hell, and they knew not God, the Judge of Deeds. They knew not the Lord God, the All-Powerful Ruler. No praise could they raise unto the Guardian of Heaven, the Wielder of Glory.

Woe betide him who, in time of suffering, shall offer his soul unto the embrace of Hellfire, for no comfort will come to him. But well will it be for him who, upon ending the days of his life, his Lord may face and find solace in his Father's embrace.

III

Thus, Hrothgar, the son of Healfdene, brooded unceasingly on his long-lasting sorrow. He could not assuage his sadness, for too painful was the anguish, awful and loathsome, the worst of night-terrors, that had befallen his folk.

From his far-off homeland, Beowulf, a thane of King Hygelac, heard tell of Grendel's depredations. This Beowulf was the greatest warrior from the tribe of Geats. Of heroes then living, he was the most strong and most stalwart, noble and fearless. Beowulf bade his men make ready a good ship. Yon battle King far o'er the swan's-road, said Beowulf, he fain would seek out, Hrothgar, the famous prince who had need of men. No wise man reproached Beowulf for undertaking this perilous journey, although dear to them was he. The omens augured well, and so they urged on the champion renowned for his courage. The valorous Beowulf then chose the boldest fighters he could find from amongst the Geats. He selected fourteen men, the bravest and the best, and led them down unto the ship resting at the shore. There a sailor skilled in the line of the coast and the currents showed them the way to the sea.

The time had come. The ship floated upon the waves, bobbing beneath the cliffs. Eager fighters clambered aboard at the prow. The tide turned, whipping the sea against the sand. The well-accoutered warriors loaded splendid war weapons and battle gear into the bosom of the vessel, and then heaved off the stout-timbered ship, sailing away on their much sought-for adventure.

They sped before the wind like a bird, cutting a foaming path through the waves, until, in due course, on the second day, the ship with the curved prow hove within sight of land, the shining sea-cliffs, towering promontories and broad headlands. Then was the sea traversed, the journey ended. Thence quickly did the Geat clansmen climb onto the ground and make fast their ship. As they did so, their armor rattled, their battle gear clattered. And then God they thanked for their passing in peace over the paths of the sea.

Now, from the cliff edge, a Danish watch-man espied them. It was this coast warden's duty to guard the sea-cliffs. He saw the Geat warriors come ashore bearing bright shining shields and war-implements in readiness. Curiosity overcame him as to what men these might be. So this thane of Hrothgar, spurring his steed, rode down unto the shore, brandishing his mighty spear and challenging them in formal words:

"What manner of soldiers be you, clad in chain-mail, who sail over the sea-road in your tall ship? For many years, I have been guardian of our coasts, standing as sea-warden, lest enemies ravish our Danish dominions with an army of war ships. Never have shield-bearing warriors so boldly ventured to come hither, lacking our kinsmen's leave and soldiers' password. Nor have I ever witnessed a greater warrior on Earth than this man standing before me, a hero in armor. He is no commoner bedecked with weapons, unless his countenance and comely appearance belie him. I pray you, though, ere you pass upon your journey as spies in the land of the Danes, tell me to what race do you belong. So now, you far-dwellers, you sea-faring sailors, hear you and hearken unto my words, haste is most fitting, speak now and tell me of whence you are come."

IV

Beowulf, the leader of the war-troop, rendered him answer, unlocking his word-hoard:

"We are sprung from the lineage of the people of Geatland, and owe obeisance to King Hygelac. My father, a noble warrior chieftain named Ecgtheow, was well known among the nations. He endured many winters, sojourning among the people, ere he passed away, an aged man. He is remembered still by wise men throughout the width and breadth of the world.

"With feelings of friendship have we come to seek your Lord and Liege, protector of his people, Hrothgar, the son of Healfdene. Counsel us well. We bear a weighty commission unto the renowned Lord of the Danes, and we shall hide naught of our undertaking.

"You will know if the truth is indeed as we have heard tell, that they say some uncouth foe, some savage despoiler, some secret pursuer, hunts and kills Danish men on dusky nights and wreaks direful destruction, malice and murder.

"To Hrothgar, wise and worthy, I therefore, with a generous spirit, offer my help to free him from this accursed destroyer, and end the anguish of his sorrow, and allow comfort once more to come unto him. Else, ever after, he must endure great hardship and distress while stands in place, high on its hill, that house unmatched."

Then spoke the coast warden, the undaunted sea-watcher, bestriding his stallion:

"The warlike shield-bearer, if he thinks well on it, must surely know the difference between words and works. This band, I hear, bears no malice toward our King Hrothgar, Lord of the Danes. I rest satisfied of your good intentions. You may proceed onward bearing weapons and war-gear, and I shall lead you in person. Further, I will bid mine own kinsmen to guard honorably your vessel against all enemies, its freshly-tarred keel upon the sand, till once again your ship with the curved prow shall carry the well-beloved hero o'er the waves of the water, back to the Kingdom of the Geats. May it be vouchsafed unto a warrior so valiant that he emerge unscathed from the fury of battle."

Onward they journeyed then. Their broad-beamed vessel floated at rest in the water, fettered by its moorings and lashed unto its anchor. Atop the gilded helmets of these soldiers shone the image of the wild boar, burnished and hardened by fire. This emblem provided protection, and watched over the lives of these men of war. Their martial spirit was fierce as they hastened on their way, till, at last, they perceived Heorot, the great-timbered, wide-gabled hall, magnificent and gold-bedecked. This was, among all the dwellings upon Earth, the most celebrated of palaces beneath the Heavens, wherein Hrothgar, the powerful prince, abided. Its noble luster illuminated lands beyond number.

Then the battle-brave coast warden pointed to the glittering court of Hrothgar's proud men, that the warriors might wend their way thither straightaway. Whereupon, the intrepid coast warden wheeled his steed about and spoke these words unto them:

"It is time now for my departure. May the Almighty Father enfold you in His protection. May He keep you safe on your mission. I must return to the sea, against hostile hordes as warden to stand."

V

The warriors marched together along the stone-paved road. Their chain-mail shirts, hard and hand-forged, gleamed in the sun-light. The linked iron rings of their armor jangled as they walked. They came unto the great hall and, there, still weary from their sea voyage, did set down their broad shields, sturdy and battle-hardened, against the wall of the building. Then the men stacked up their spears, pikes of ash-wood with points of grey iron, the weapons of these sea-faring warriors. As they sat upon the benches, the battle armor of these heroes clattered and clanged. That iron-clad troop was worthy of its weapons.

Then a proud warrior questioned the champions of combat as to their lineage:

"Whence bear you these burnished shields, these chain-mail shirts, these visored helmets, these war-lances? I am Hrothgar's herald and liegeman. My name is Wulfgar. Never have I met so many strangers of a more stalwart mien. From heroic valor and greatness of soul, so I imagine, do you seek out King Hrothgar, and not because of banishment."

The Prince of the Geats, renowned for his courage, made answer to him:

"We break bread with King Hygelac at his table. I am called Beowulf. I shall relate my mission unto the illustrious Prince, your Lord Hrothgar, the son of Healfdene, if he will grant us leave to greet him, so good a man as he is."

Then Wulfgar made reply. He was a Prince of the Vandals. His boldness of spirit, bravery in battle and wisdom was well-known to many. "I will fain tell Hrothgar, the King of the Danes, the giver of rings, the renowned Prince, of your coming hither, as you have urged me to do. Swiftly thereafter, such answer shall I bring unto you as our noble Prince may deign to give."

Then turned Wulfgar in haste and hied to where Hrothgar sat, aged and hoary, amidst his band of Earls. Wulfgar, the warrior famed for his valor, knew the custom of the court. He went forward and stood squarely at the shoulder of the King of the Danes.

Wulfgar addressed then his benevolent Liege Lord, thus:

"Hither have come men from Geatland. They have sailed from afar over the expanse of the ocean. These champions of battle call their chieftain by the name of Beowulf. They are suppliants, my Prince, who seek an exchange of words with you. O gracious King Hrothgar, refuse not to render them friendly answer. From their weapons and armor, methinks, they appear worthy of the esteem of noblemen. Indeed, Beowulf, the leader who carried these soldiers to our shores is a mighty and valiant hero."

VI

Hrothgar, protector of the Danes, spoke in reply:

"I knew Beowulf when he was the merest of striplings. His father, now long dead, was named Ecgtheow. Unto Ecgtheow did Hrethel, King of the Geats, give in marriage his only daughter. This Beowulf is their offspring. Now the battle-brave son of Ecgtheow is come hither to greet a steadfast friend. Seafaring sailors, who bore our tribute of rich gifts unto the Geats, have said to me that Beowulf, bold in battle, has the strength of thirty men in the grip of each hand. It is my hope that our Holy God, in His mercy, has sent Beowulf unto us, the Danes, to protect us against the horror of Grendel. I shall offer generous treasure to this valorous warrior for his gallant intent. Hasten to bid that throng of Geat kinsmen to come hither and stand before me. And, tell them also, that they are welcome guests of the Danish folk."

Then Wulfgar went to the door of the hall and this word-message shouted out unto the Geats:

"My victorious Liege Lord, Prince of the Danes, bade me tell you that he knows your lineage. He says that you are welcome here, valiant men from afar o'er the surge of the sea. Now may you enter the great hall in your helmets and war attire to see King Hrothgar. But your battle shields and spears, deadly war shafts, must remain outside the great hall, awaiting the outcome of your discourse."

Beowulf, the powerful one, arose then, as did the warriors about him, a superb band of soldiers. Some there did abide, as their courageous chief commanded them, to keep guard over their battle gear. Then Beowulf and his men hastened to where the herald did guide them, under Heorot's high roof, into the presence of Hrothgar. Beowulf, heroic under his helmet, his chain mail shirt shining, proof of the art of the armorer, went forward till he stood at the hearth, and then spoke these words:

"Hail to you, Hrothgar. I am kinsman and vassal to King Hygelac. I have, in my youth, undertaken many renowned deeds. The ravages of Grendel heard I in my home-land heralded clear. Seafarers say how stands this hall, this excellent edifice, for your band of thanes, empty and useless, when evening sun has hidden its glory 'neath Heaven's firmament. Then, O King Hrothgar, did my vassals counsel me, the noblest and wisest of them, that I should come hither to seek you out and assist you, for my might they knew full well. They themselves had beheld me, bathed in the blood of my enemies, when I came back from the battle in the darkness of night. There I desolated the lair of the race of ogres and enchained five of them and slew sea-beasts uncounted amid the murky depths of the waves. I avenged the wrong done to the Geats, for they had suffered many woes, and I destroyed their foes. Their enemies deserved their Fate.

"And now, in single combat, shall I settle the matter with that monster of evil, and quell the demon Grendel. Now then, O Prince of the Danes, protector of the people, I will entreat of you but one boon. Refuse me not, defender of warriors, noble friend to the folk, since I have wandered so far. Grant that I and my company of liegemen, this band of brave soldiers, may purge Heorot unaided. Furthermore have I also learned that the reckless wretch, Grendel, disdains weapons of warfare. Hence shall I also scorn sword and shield, in order to gladden the heart of my beloved King Hygelac. With my bare hands alone will I grapple with the adversary and fight to the death, foe against foe. He whom Death shall take must needs trust to the judgment of the Lord.

"Indeed, methinks, if Grendel does prevail in this struggle, he intends to devour my band of Geats in this hall of gold, as oft before he did to your warriors. If Death must overtake me, you will have no need to bury me, for Grendel's shall I be, all bestained in gore. He will carry off my bloody body and gorge himself without remorse on my remains and turn his lair in the fen red with my life-blood. Therefore, lament and bewail not for the care of my corpse. If I should fall in combat, send unto my King Hygelac this best of battle garments, this armor that serves to shield my bosom, the richest of ring-mail. It is my heritage from Hrethel, the hand-work of Weland, the most skillful of smiths.

"Fate will do as she must."

VII

Then spoke Hrothgar, the protector of the Danes:

"Beowulf, my good friend, you have kindly sought us hither to succor us and save us, to defend our folk in battle. Your father enkindled the fiercest of feuds when, with his own hand, he slew Heatholaf, a Wylfing warrior. Then your father's race, the Geats, for fear of further fighting, were forced to disown him. Fleeing, he sailed over the surging seas unto the land of the Danes, the men of honor. That was when I had lately begun to govern the Danes. I was then but a youth ruling this wide-spread realm, a stronghold of heroes. By then, my elder brother, Heorogar, the first son of Healfdene, had breathed his last. He was a better man than I am. Afterwards, the feud with blood-money I settled. I sent ancient treasures over the waves of the water to the Wylfings. Your father, then, swore oaths of allegiance unto me.

"There is sorrow in my soul for me to tell any man of what grief Grendel, in his enmity and sudden onslaughts, has caused us in Heorot, and of our humiliation. The numbers of my palace-band, my war-troop are diminished. Fate has swept them away, into the clutches of Grendel. Surely, God could foil this mischievous foe from his deeds so direful.

"Full often have warriors, drunk with beer, boasted over their ale-cups that they would bide here in the hall to await Grendel's assault with sharpened swords. Then, at morning tide, when daylight broke, this mead-hall was red with gore, the boards of the benches blood-besoaked. I had fewer faithful retainers, dear-beloved companions, for Death had carried them off.

"Sit you now to the feast, Beowulf, and joyfully eat, while relating unto us your valiant exploits, as your spirit may prompt you."

Then, in the great mead-hall, a bench was made ready for the men of the Geats together assembled. There, sturdy of spirit, the men went to be seated, exceeding proud and exultant. A thane attended them, pouring out draughts of the sweet mead from an adorned ale-cup. At times, a minstrel chanted in a bright clear voice, hearty in Heorot. Heroes rejoiced, Geats and Danes, and the warriors sang as one.

VIII

Unferth, the son of Ecglaf, spoke out then. This thane sat at the feet of the Danish king. Sorely vexed, he would dispute with Beowulf. The sturdy sea-farer's journey caused Unferth great bitterness, for he granted not that any man under Heaven might gain greater glory than he himself held.

"Are you that Beowulf who strove against Breca, contending upon the wide waves of the ocean sea for foolish pride, risking your life-days in the briny deeps for the sake of a vainglorious boast? Nor could any living man, friend or foe, in the least dissuade you from your unwise adventure, ere you swam out to the depths. There you two plied the ocean streams with the strokes of your arms, you took the measure of the sea with strenuous hands, you glided o'er the watery ways. The deep sea raged with rough waves, with winter's swell. In the realm of the sea, you swam for the space of seven nights. Breca outmatched you in swimming. In strength, he excelled you. Then, early at morning-tide on the eighth day, the sea bore him up unto the coast of Norway. Thence, he sought his own paternal country, dear to his liegemen, the land of the Brondings, where he ruled over a people, a castle fair and treasure untold.

"In triumph over you, Breca fulfilled his boast. Therefore, although hitherto, you have been victorious in combat and grim battle, if you dare abide near unto Grendel for the duration of a night, I expect a less fortunate outcome."

Then Beowulf, the son of Ecgtheow, spoke:

"Lo, my friend Unferth, drunk as you are with beer, you have uttered many words about Breca. You have told of his triumph. But I count it as truth that I had greater strength in the sea, more endurance in the ocean, than any other man.

"We twain had talked and boasted, Breca and I, in the time of our youth, striplings still, that we would venture our lives out upon the ocean, and so we performed this deed. While swimming the sea-floods, we both brandished an unsheathed sword, to shield us against the whale-fishes. Not a whit could he outpace me o'er the waves of the water, or swim more rapidly than me, nor would I consent to part from him. Together we two on the tides floated full five nights, till the flood forced us apart. The surging sea, the coldest of winters, the darkling night and the brutal North wind turned against us. Rough was the wrath of the billows.

"Now was the anger of the sea-beasts aroused. Yet did my shirt of chain-mail, hard and hand-linked, afford me protection against my foes. My woven war-weeds, garnished with gold, lay upon my chest. A fierce, hateful sea-monster seized me and dragged me down to the depths. The grim beast held me fast in its grip. 'Twas granted me, though, to pierce the sea-fiend, through and through, with the point of my battle-sword. That formidable beast of the sea was overwhelmed by the force of my hand.

IX

"Thus oft and oft over did malicious enemies violently menace me. I dealt them due return with the thrust of my dear sword, as it was fitting. These foul sea-beasts would not have the pleasure of feasting abundantly upon my body at the bottom of the sea. Yea, rather, at morning-tide, these cursed creatures, butchered by my blade, put to sleep by the stroke of my sword, were stretched out upon the sand of the shore. Never since have they hindered the passage of sea-farers upon their voyage over the fathomless flood.

"Came the light from the Eastward, the bright beacon of God, and grew the seas calm. Then well could I perceive sea-cliffs high, wind-swept crags. For Fate oft saves a man not yet doomed to die, if he be dauntless. And so it befell me that I had the good Fortune to slay nine sea-monsters with my sword. Never heard I of a battle harder fought by night 'neath Heaven's high arc, nor adrift upon the deep a more hard-pressed man. Nevertheless, did I escape with my life, unharmed, though spent from swimming. Then the sea, the flood, the raging surges of the waves cast me ashore upon the coast of Finland.

"Not a word has been related unto me of deeds so daring done by you, Unferth, nothing of clashing sword-terror. I boast not of the struggle, but neither you nor Breca, on the field of battle, with shining sword, such daring deed has done at all. Moreover, you were the killer of your brothers, your nearest of kin. For this, you shall suffer direful Damnation in the depths of Hell, no matter how sharp your wit may be. I, furthermore, affirm to you in truth, Unferth, son of Ecglaf, that Grendel, that wicked wretch, would never have wrought so many horrors against your Prince, wreaked so much havoc in Heorot, if your heart and your spirit were as undaunted in warfare as you have accounted them to be. But the beast has learned he need not fear that a feud will follow, that he need not dread the terrible sword-vengeance of your clan, the victorious Danes. The monster takes his toll and shows no mercy unto any Dane. He lustily fights and feasts on Danish flesh, expecting no opposition and no retribution.

"But shortly now shall I show him the Geat's strength and steadfastness in battle. Then, after the struggle, when comes the light of dawn, and the Sun shall shine from the Southward over the children of men, he who is able may go high-hearted to mead-drinking."

Then was glad the giver of treasure, Hrothgar, grey-haired and brave in battle. The protector of his people, the Prince of the Danes, trusted in the pledge and firm resolve of Beowulf. The loud laughter of the liegemen resounded through the hall, the sounds of winsome words.

Whereupon Wealhtheow, Hrothgar's queen, gold-bedecked, came forth and, heedful of courtesy, saluted the warriors in the building. The high-born Lady first gave the goblet of mead unto the guardian of the Danes, her husband, and bade him be blithe at the banquet, he who was beloved by his people. The war-renowned ruler joyfully received the beaker and blessed the banquet. Then Wealhtheow graciously circled the assemblage from warrior to warrior, proffering the precious cup to young and old alike, until, at last, she bore the beaker of mead unto Beowulf. The ring-bedecked, noble-hearted Queen greeted the Prince of the Geats and, wise in her words, did give thanks unto God that her wish had been fulfilled, that she might trust in some hero for solace in sorrow.

Beowulf, courageous in combat, took the goblet from Wealhtheow's hand and, eager for battle, would speak some words.

Beowulf, son of Ecgtheow, spoke thus:

"When I and my troop of warriors set out in my ship upon the deep sea, I resolved that I should fully carry out the will of your people or fall in fighting, fast in the grip of that foul fiend. I am firm in my determination to accomplish this deed of heroic valor, or else end the days of my life in this mead-hall."

These words, Beowulf's battle boast, pleased the woman well. And so the free-born Queen of the people, her garment embroidered with gold, went to sit by the side of her spouse. Then were again, as of yore, proud words and the cheering of warriors heard within the hall, the revels of heroes. Then Hrothgar, the son of Healfdene, rose to seek his slumber. He knew that war awaited in the high hall, a fight against the fiend, when they saw no longer the sheen of the sun, and lowering darkness was descended over all, and shadowy shapes should come stealing forth, black beneath the clouds. The warriors arose. Then Hrothgar saluted Beowulf and wished him well, and gave Heorot unto his care and keeping, and spoke these words:

"Never before, since my hand could lift a shield, have I entrusted this excellent hall of the Danes to any man, save now unto you. Take charge now and guard this noblest of houses. Be mindful of fame, display steadfast courage, keep watch for the foe. You shall want no treasure should you emerge from this heroic task with boldly-won life."

X

Then did Hrothgar, protector of the Danes, depart out of the hall with his band of heroes. Fain would the war-leader seek the bed of his queen, Wealhtheow, to lie with her. As men have heard recounted, God Himself against Grendel had provided Beowulf as a defender of the hall, to guard the monarch and maintain vigilant watch for the monster. Verily did Beowulf, Prince of the Geats, trust in his mettle, his might and the mercy of the Creator. His armor of iron he cast off then, and his helmet from his head, and gave them unto his henchman. He bid the thane to safeguard well this battle-gear, together with his ornamented sword, the choicest of weapons.

And then the valorous warrior, Beowulf of the Geats, ere he sought his bed, spoke some boastful words:

"I account myself no less accomplished in war-strength, in battle-deeds, than Grendel deems himself. Hence, not with a sword shall I slay him, despoil him of life, though it easily lies in my power to do so. No battle-skill has he, although he may strike against my sword and hew at my shield, and albeit he be renowned for works of malice. I will, this night, meet him without sword, if he dare seek warfare without weapons. Let God in His infinite wisdom, the Holy Lord, apportion glory to whomsoever He chooses."

Then the battle-brave hero bent to his slumber; his pillow received the nobleman's cheek. All about him, the hardy sea-farers on hall-beds rested their heads. Not a man believed he should ever again behold his beloved land, his brethren or his high-walled burg. They had heard full well that many warriors of the Danish clan had been carried off to their battle-deaths in that hallowed mead-hall. But God's great loom had woven a weft and warp of help for the Geats, and victory in battle. Through the might of one man, by his strength, would they all prevail against their adversary. Thus, was the truth made manifest that Almighty God has ever ruled over mankind.

Out of the blackest of nights prowled Grendel, the shadowy stalker. All the warriors, whose task it was to guard the gabled hall, were asleep. All, save one. It was well known unto men that, if the Lord were unwilling, the spectral avenger was powerless to hurl them down into the depths of darkness.

But Beowulf, wakeful and wrathful, eagerly awaited the enemy, and the outcome of the conflict.

XI

Then, under the veils of fog, past misty crags, came Grendel from the moor. Upon his back he bore the burden of God's wrath. The monster was mindful of men now, purposed to seize and devour his prey in Heorot, that high hall. Beneath the cloud cover, the beast skulked silently till he perceived most clearly that magnificent hall, the treasure house of heroes, flashing with gilded fretwork. This was not the first time he had sought out Hrothgar's home, yet never before, in all his life-days, had he found such ill Fortune and such stalwart foes.

The creature, bereft of contentment for all time, came unto the hall. Whereupon, the door, fastened with fire-forged fetters, quickly sprang open when his hands struck it. With baleful rage, intent on malice, the fiend flung the door ajar and swiftly stepped upon the fair inlaid floor. From his eyes streamed forth fearful flashes, very like unto flames. Within the hall, he espied many a warrior sleeping, a throng of thanes. Then his heart was exultant. The grim beast determined, ere day should dawn, to sever the soul from the body of each, for a lusty banquet awaited his will.

But Fate, that night, forbade him ever again to feast upon the flesh of men.

Exceeding strong, Beowulf, the kinsman of Hygelac, beheld how the raging beast would proceed with his sudden onslaught. No thought had the monster of tarrying in his attack. Straightaway he seized a sleeping warrior and tore him fiercely asunder. The creature bit his bones, breaking them, swallowed his blood in streams and gorged on great chunks of his body. Swiftly thus was the lifeless corpse devoured, even unto the hands and feet.

Then the beast strode forward and tried to grasp with fiendish claws the hardy hero in his bed. But, ere he could do so, Beowulf reached out and caught the foe with his mighty hand. Soon did the master of malice discover that he had never met, upon the face of the Earth, in no far corner of the world, a harder hand-grip in any man. The monster grew heart-fearful, for he could not break free. His spirit would fain flee, to run unto his lair, to seek the assembly of devils. His plight, on that night, was such as he had not met with, in all the days of his life.

Then Beowulf, loyal liegeman of Hygelac, bethought himself of his evening speech. Up he bounded and further tightened his grip upon the foe, till the monster's claws cracked. The beast stepped back, the hero stepped forward. The infamous creature fought for his freedom, to fly away thence to his fen-dwelling. He knew his claws were powerless in the grip of the wrathful warrior. 'Twas an ill-Fated trip the terrible ravager had taken unto Heorot.

A thunderous din filled the noble hall. Dread overcame the Danes, the hall-dwellers, clansmen all. Both antagonists were angry, raging and mighty. The building resounded with the clash of combat. It was a marvelous wonder that the mighty hall withstood the fearsome battle-blows, that it fell not to the ground. But it was firmly braced, both within and without, with bands of iron, artfully forged by a skilled smith. Where the grim foes wrestled, many a mead bench, adorned with gold-work, as I have heard tell, was knocked off its base. Ere this time, Hrothgar's counselors had never believed that any man might wreck that noble hall in any manner, unless the embrace of fire should engulf it in flames.

Again and again arose a new noise, surpassing strange. A fearful terror came upon the Danes, all the men there in the hall who heard the outcry, heard the enemy of God sing his dreadful lay, his song of defeat, howling his hymns of Hell, bewailing his wound. He who was the mightiest of men in the days of this life held the beast too fast in the bonds of death.

XII

Beowulf, defender of the warriors, would not suffer the slaughtering stranger to depart alive. He did not deem the demon's life as useful to any man.

Now many of Beowulf's band brandished their ancestral battle blades. Fain would they shield the life of their Lord, their much-praised Prince, if they could. Waging this warfare, these sturdy soldiers struck Grendel from every side, seeking to end his life. But they knew not that the finest war sword in the world, the keenest piece of iron fashioned upon Earth, could never pierce the evil monster, for he had bewitched their weapons and rendered their swords of no avail.

And, yet, Grendel's parting from life at this time was doomed to be wretched, for his hateful spirit would be hurled down into Hell, into the hands of hard-hearted fiends. The demon plainly saw then, he who, in former days, wicked by nature and hated by God, had gladly harassed the hearts of men, that his strength would no longer serve him. For Beowulf, Hygelac's bold kinsman, had him fast in his grasp. Now was each hateful to the other, as long as either breathed life. The direful demon suffered great hurt. A huge gash was seen on his shoulder. His sinews snapped. His bones burst and broke. His arm was sundered from his body. Unto Beowulf now was glory in battle bestowed.

Grendel, mortally wounded, thence must needs flee unto the bog and fen to seek his joyless den. He knew but too well that the last of his life was come, the full measure of his days was at hand.

By this bloody battle, the desire of all the Danes was done. The undaunted warrior who had newly come from afar, wise and valiant, had purged the high hall of Hrothgar, had secured it from harm. His night-work pleased him, his deed of heroic valor. The Prince of the Geat warriors had fulfilled his boast unto the Danes. He had assuaged all their sorrows and anguish, which they were forced to endure and suffer through dire necessity. That was no little misfortune. Then was displayed manifest proof of his victory when the battle-brave hero nailed, unto the wall, the whole of Grendel's grip, hung high in Heorot hall—the claw, the arm, the shoulder all.

XIII

And then, in the mist of morning, as I have heard, many a warrior gathered round that gift-hall. Clan leaders, from far and near, travelled over distant roads to behold that wonder, the foot-prints of the foe. None who gazed upon the tracks of the inglorious demon lamented his departure from life. The beast, weary and heart-sick, beaten in battle, defeated and driven to flight, left behind him proof of his life-blood ebbing as he made his way unto the lake of the water-monsters. There, the water boiled with bloody billows, the foul tide of tumbling waves seethed with hot gore, surged with sword-blood. Then the fiend, death-doomed, bereft of joy, laid his forlorn life down, his heathen soul, in that marsh den. And there did Hell receive him.

Thence again the old clansmen returned, and many a young man also, on that merry journey from the lake, high-spirited warriors upon stallions. Then were proclaimed praises of Beowulf's glory. All affirmed that nowhere in the wide world, neither Northward nor Southward between the two seas, 'neath the course of the Sun, was there any warrior bearing a shield more worthy of Kingship, more noble than he. Of their beloved friend and Lord, gracious Hrothgar, they meant no slight, for he was a good King.

From time to time, those famed in battle set their sorrel steeds to gallop together and run a race, when the fields to them seemed fair and inviting.

And, from time to time, the King's thane, a man well-versed in rhythms, mindful of many sagas of valiant exploits, bound word unto word in well-wrought rime to craft a new tale. The bard skillfully began to frame the deeds of Beowulf and relate the history of this hero. He also recited all he had heard of the old saga of Sigemund, of his courageous feats, of many a strange adventure, of the struggles of the son of Waels, and of his wide wayfarings. He sang of the feuds and felonies unknown to the children of men, save to Fitela only, when suchlike matters Sigemund had a mind to speak of, as uncle to nephew. The twain had ever, in friendship, stood side by side in the stress of battle. With their swords they had felled very many of the race of giants. To Sigemund accrued no little glory when his life-days were done, for, brave in battle, he had slain a Dragon, guardian of the treasure-hoard.

As the story goes, Sigemund, son of a Prince, had adventured unaided 'neath the grey cliff on that perilous project. Nor was Fitela there. Yet, good Fortune befell him, for his sword, worthy weapon, pierced the monstrous Dragon and pinned it unto the wall. The Dragon was slaughtered by that mighty blow.

Thus by his daring did Sigemund, the undaunted one, gain possession of that treasure-hoard of rings to rule at his will. Sigemund, the son of Waels, did then load a sea-boat and fill its hold with gleaming gold. The Dragon was consumed by flames.

No wanderer was more widely renowned among world-folk, this protector of warriors, for deeds of courage. Sigemund's fame and his wealth grew great.

In times past, after the hand and heart of Heremod grew slack in battle, this once proud and mighty King of the Danes was banished unto the hands of his enemies in Jutland, where he was betrayed and speedily put to death. Surges of sorrow had too long oppressed Heremod. Unto his despondent people, unto all the disheartened nobles, he became an ever-greater burden. Oft indeed, in earlier days, many a wise man was wont to deplore the deeds of the cruel-hearted Heremod. These selfsame sages had believed in him as a bulwark against harm and evil. They had thought that the son of a ruler should rise unto power, follow his father's footsteps, protect the people, its treasure-hoard and stronghold, the realm of heroes, the homeland of the Danes. All this Heremod, wicked King, failed to do.

Beowulf, liegeman of Hygelac, to all kindred and races became more fair, more beloved. But Heremod was inclined to malice and wrongdoing.

Once more, racing upon their swift steeds, the warriors took the measure of the roads. The morning sun rose and brightened the ways. Many a man, bold in spirit, hastened unto the high-built hall to witness the wonder. And then King Hrothgar himself, keeper of the ring-hoard, renowned for his virtues, stepped forth glorious from his wife's chamber, accompanied by a great troop of his courtiers. With him, the Queen-wife, Wealhtheow, went, attended by her company of maidens, and they all walked unto the mead-hall.

XIV

Hrothgar stood upon the step and looked up at the steep roof shining with gold and saw Grendel's arm. Then he spoke:

"For this sight we now behold, thanks be speedily rendered unto the Almighty. Much evil have I endured, many sorrows at the hand of Grendel. But God, Guardian of Glory, does work wonder after wonder. It was not long since when I despaired deeply of ever finding succor from my woes as long as I drew breath. Heorot, the best of houses, stood blood bestained and splattered with sword-gore. Woe was wide-spread among the wise men, who felt they could not defend this fortress of warriors against our foes, against wicked demons and fiendish phantoms. But now has a dauntless warrior, through the power of God, accomplished a feat which erstwhile all of us could not contrive to do with our wiles and cunning. Lo! Whatsoever woman bore such a son among mankind, if she yet lives, she may say that the Creator was gracious unto her in child-birth.

"Now, Beowulf, most excellent of heroes, I shall esteem you in my heart as mine own son. Preserve you henceforward this new kinship. You will never lack aught you desire of world-goods which are mine to command. Full oft for less have I showered largesse upon a weaker warrior, less stalwart in struggle. You, yourself, have, by your deeds, ensured that your glory will endure forever and ever. May the Almighty always requite you with good from His hand, as He has hitherto done you."

Beowulf, son of Ecgtheow, spoke:

"We, most willingly, accomplished that daring deed, that bold battle, against the force of the unknown foe. Fain would I that you had beheld the beast, weary unto decease, about to fall. In all haste, I meant to bring him down, grapple with him until his death-agony, so that, unless he should slip my grip, his days would end in my arms. But I could not. The Lord did not will it so. I did not hold the deadly destroyer firmly enough. Too strong was he, and too swift. Yet, to save his life, he suffered his claw, arm and shoulder to remain behind. But the woe-begone creature found no solace by that, for the malicious fiend is freighted down with sins. He will live no longer. The wound has already clutched him in its fatal grasp, in baleful bonds. There he must bide, stained by sin, awaiting the Final Judgment, whatever awful doom the God of Glory shall mete out unto him."

Then was Unferth, son of Ecglaf, silent in boasting of his battle-deeds, when the hall-thanes perceived proof of the Prince's power. Beneath the lofty hall-timbers, they beheld Grendel's huge hand hanging down, each finger-nail as strong as steel, the heathen's hand-spear, the beast's most uncanny claw. 'Twas clear, they all agreed, that no time-tested blade of brave men, no matter how keen, could ever dissever the monster's bloody battle-claw from his body.

XV

Then Hrothgar commanded that Heorot be adorned within by all hands. Whereupon, a host gathered, many men and women, to prepare that wine-hall, the house of guests to garnish. On the walls, tapestries gleamed with woven gold threads, a wondrous sight for all mortals who look upon such. But that glorious palace, despite its iron buttresses, was very much broken, its hinges rent apart. The roof alone survived unscathed, when the fiendish foe, guilty of crime-deeds, despairing of life, his flight assayed. However, Death is not easy to flee from—let him attempt it who will. Every one who has life, every one of the sons of men, every one possessed of a soul, as Fate has decreed, must needs seek out the death-bed awaiting him, wherein the flesh shall sleep for all Eternity after the feast of life is finished.

Arrived was the hour and season befitting that Hrothgar, son of Healfdene, should go unto the hall. The King himself would partake of the feast. Never did I hear of a more noble throng graciously gathered about their treasure-giver. These men of renown then sat upon the benches and rejoiced in the banquet. Now those kinsmen, Hrothgar and Hrothulf, his nephew, in seemly fashion, drank of many a mead-goblet in that lofty gabled hall. Heorot at that time was filled with friends. Not then did the race of Danes embrace the arts of deceitfulness and treachery, as they later would.

Then did Hrothgar, son of Healfdene, give unto Beowulf, as tokens of triumph, a battle-ensign embroidered with gold, a helmet, and a coat of chain-mail. And many a man saw the famous splendid sword borne as a tribute unto the brave one. Beowulf quaffed the mead-goblet in the high hall. He suffered no shame in being showered with such rich gifts before those soldiers. Never heard I of many men, upon the mead-bench, giving four such treasures, fashioned with gold, in such a generous spirit. Across the crest of the helmet, a ridge wound with wire bands guarded the hero's head, so that no battle-hardened sword would harm him when the shield-bearing warrior was destined to fight against fierce foes.

And then Hrothgar, the defender of warriors, ordered that eight stallions with gold bridles be brought unto the hall. Upon one of the steeds lay a saddle, artfully adorned and bejeweled. That was the war-seat the exalted King Hrothgar rode upon whenever he wished to engage in sword-play. Never failed his valor in the clash of combat when his faithful followers were falling upon the field of battle.

Upon Beowulf did Hrothgar then bestow both war-steeds and weapons. He bade Beowulf use them well. Thus, in so manfully a manner did the mighty King, the treasure-keeper of heroes, reward that hard-fought contest with horses and valuables. No man who utters the truth will ever speak ill of them.

XVI

Moreover, Hrothgar, the leader of warriors, gave unto each of them who had made the sea-journey with Beowulf a costly gift-token, an heirloom. He ordered that gold be paid in recompense for the Geat whom Grendel had so maliciously murdered. And the monster would have killed more of them had not omniscient God and one man's courage that Fate did avert. The Creator has ever ruled over mankind, and will ever do so. Hence insight, prudence of thought, is always most fitting. He who sojourns long in this woeful world shall encounter much of joy and sorrow.

There was music and merriment mingled together in the presence of Hrothgar, Heorot's chieftain. The happy harp was plucked. Upon the mead-bench, the King's minstrel sang the oft-sung saga of Finn, King of the Frisians, and his sons:

Hnaef, hero of the Danes, was destined to fall upon the Frisian battle-field when the sudden onslaught of Finn's warriors overcame him. His sister, Finn's wife, Hildeburh, had no cause to praise the fidelity of the Frisians. She was blameless, but she was bereft of both brother and son on that battle-day. Mortally wounded by war-spear, they fell to their Fate. She was a mournful woman. Not in vain did she lament her loss when dawning came and she beheld, beneath the Heavens, her slain kinsmen, when hitherto she had known the sweetest bliss in the world.

By this battle also were carried away most of Finn's own liegemen, save for a few. Thus Finn could no longer fight to the finish against Hengest, new leader of the Danes. And he could not rescue by means of warfare his wretched remnant of warriors.

Therefore, a pact was proposed. The Danes and the Frisians would share of power equally, of hall and throne. At the bestowal of fee-gifts, Finn should honor the Danes, day by day, granting unto Hengest's soldiers precious rings, treasures of wrought-gold, as he would honor his own men in that mead-hall.

On both sides then they pledged a fast-binding peace compact. Finn plighted unto Hengest, with undisputed solemn oath, that he would treat the survivors of the conflict honorably, in accord with the judgment of his wise men. They agreed that no man, by word or deed, should break the truce, nor, with malice, ever recall the quarrel or bemoan the fact that they were compelled to follow their ring-giver's slayer. This necessity was forced upon them by Fate. Moreover, if any of the Frisians should speak of the deadly clash in taunting tones, the edge of Finn's sword would answer that insolent speech.

The funeral pyre was then prepared. A treasure of gold was borne up from the hoard. The best of warriors were laid upon the pyre, awaiting the flames. Blood-stained shirts of chain-mail were clearly seen, and golden helmets with images of wild boars, hard as iron. Many a high-born kinsman, slain by sword, lay thereon, fallen in battle.

Then Hildeburh bade her own son to be given over to the fire, upon Hnaef's funeral pyre. His body would be consumed by the flames, side by side with his uncle, Hildeburh's brother. The woman wailed and keened, sang mournful death dirges. The warriors ascended to Heaven in battle-smoke. The greatest of death-fires curled upward toward the clouds, whilst the roaring of the flames resounded forth from the burial-mound. Heads were a-melting, gaping wounds split open and burst, blood coursed out. And then the fire, greediest of spirits, devoured all those of both peoples whom war had taken. Their glory was departed.

XVII

Bereaved of their friends, Finn's warriors left to go unto their dwellings and strongholds, to see their Frisian homeland. Hengest, who was disconsolate, continued biding peaceably with Finn through the whole of that blood-tainted winter. Yet of home he thought endlessly, though powerless was he to sail his ring-prowed ship over the sea. For the storm-driven waves surged, whipped by the winds. Winter bound them, land-locked them within fetters of ice.

Then came another year to the dwellings of men, as it does still unto this day. The season of sun-shine, of bright lustrous light, was at hand. Far away was winter driven. Fair then was the Earth's bosom.

Hengest, the exile, longed to leave the land of the Frisians. But, rather, he pondered more upon vengeance than upon voyage. He wished to hasten the onset of a hostile encounter by which he might wreak his revenge upon the sons of the Frisians. But Hengest avoided not death when a liegeman of Finn plunged into his breast the famed battle-sword, Flame of War, the best of blades. Its edges were renowned among the followers of Finn.

Whereupon, the Danish warriors bewailed the cowardly assault and fell upon the bold-hearted Finn, killing him where he bode in his own palace. It was a harsh sword-death. The Danes were wrathful, and blamed Finn for their woes and the murder of their King. Their enraged hearts could not be restrained. Then did the hall run red with the blood of enemies. Finn's corpse lay amid those of his clansmen. The Queen was taken. Unto their vessels the Danish warriors bore all the household wealth and chattels which they could find in the palace of Finn, King of the land of the Frisians, all the finely-wrought gold and jewels and treasures. Over the paths of the sea, the sailors carried the high-born Queen Hildeburh back to her Danish homeland, home unto her people.

The minstrel's song, the saga, was sung. Then glad rose the revel among the guests. Joyous sounds issued forth from those seated upon the benches. Cup-bearers poured wine from wondrous goblets. Then did Wealhtheow, noble Queen, wearing a crown of gold, enter and go to where those two good men, Hrothgar and Hrothulf, uncle and nephew, did sit. As yet, there was peace and amity between them, each true unto the other. There also was Unferth, the spokesman, who sat at the feet of his King, Hrothgar. They all trusted Unferth's spirit and said he had great courage, though he had been dishonorable in the slaying of his brothers.

Then spoke Wealhtheow, Queen of the Danes, unto Hrothgar, her husband:

"Receive this cup, my Lord, bestower of treasure. May happiness attend you, gold-giver of warriors. Speak unto the Geats with kind words, as it is fitting to do. Be gracious unto the Geats. In the giving of gifts, be not niggardly. Men say to me that you wish to take this battle-brave hero unto your breast as a son to you. Now is Heorot, bright ring-hall, cleansed because of him. Be generous with much largesse, while you still may, and then bequeath your subjects and realm unto your kinsmen when you must needs go forth to face your Fate in your final hour.

"Gracious I deem your nephew, my Hrothulf. I know he will treat your sons honorably, should you, friend of the Danes, depart from this world ere he does. I reckon that recompense he shall render unto our sons with kindness, when he does recall all that we did for him, for his pleasure and honor, when he was but a helpless child."

Then she turned toward the bench upon which her two sons, Hrethric and Hrothmund, and the sons of the other warriors were seated, young men together. There also sat the dauntless one, Beowulf of the Geats, betwixt the brothers twain.

XVIII

Unto Beowulf was a cup offered, with warm greetings and winsome words. Also wrought gold was graciously given unto Beowulf, a pair of golden arm-bands, a chain-mail shirt, gold rings, and the most magnificent neck-collar I have ever heard men speak about upon the face of the Earth. Never did I know of a greater treasure-hoard of heroes 'neath Heaven since Hama stole the neck-chain of the Brosings, with its jewels and finely-worked settings, and carried it unto his glorious stronghold. He fled from the treachery and hostility of Eormenric, thereby ensuring his everlasting gain.

Next did King Hygelac of the Geats, grandson of Swerting, possess that bejeweled neck-chain on his last foray. Beneath his banner, he defended that treasure, the booty of battle. Fate did carry him away when, from hubris, he sought a fight against the Franks and suffered misfortune. The steadfast sovereign wore that fairest of neck-chains as he sailed o'er the waves of the water. Under his shield he died. The corpse of the King fell unto the keeping of the Franks. They took his breast-armor and that glorious neck-chain. Less-noble warriors plundered the fallen after the carnage of war. The bodies of the Geat fighters had final possession of that field of battle.

A din arose in the hall.

Queen Wealhtheow spoke. She addressed the company and said:

"This neck-chain enjoy you, beloved Beowulf. Wear it with good Fortune, O young man. Use this armor, treasure of the people, and prosper well ever after. Show yourself to be strong, and be kind in counsel unto these boys. I shall not forget to reward you for that. You have accomplished such deeds that men, far and near, shall sing your praises for ages to come. You have acquired renown as wide as the seas, the home of the winds, which encircle the headlands. May you be fortunate, my Prince, for as long as you shall draw breath. I entreat for you untold riches. Be gracious in deeds unto my sons, you who possesses contentment. Here in this hall each warrior is true unto the other, all temperate in spirit, all loyal to the leader of men. The thanes are united, the people ready, the warriors wine-drunk and prepared for battle. I beseech you, do as I bid you."

Then she went unto her seat. That was the finest of feasts. The warriors drank wine. They knew not the grim Fate that awaited them. They knew not the dark Destiny that would come to these warriors after night had fallen and King Hrothgar had departed unto his chamber, the mighty majesty to his bed. Heorot, the high hall, was watched over by warriors unnumbered, as they were wont to do in days past. The men cleared away the bench-boards, and spread out bedding and bolsters. One of the revelers, doomed to die, lay down upon his bed in the hall. At their heads, they set their shining war-shields. On the bench over each warrior could be clearly seen his battle-helmet, his ring-mail shirt, and his mighty spear. It was their custom to be ever prepared for battle, both at home and on the march, at all such times as distress might befall their Liege Lord. They were a worthy people.

XIX

They sank then into sleep. One of the warriors paid dearly for his evening repose, as oftentimes had befallen before when Grendel laid waste unto the gold-hall and wrought Evil therein, till his end was upon him, Death for his sins. Later, it came to be known, widely spoken of among men, that a revenger yet outlived the loathed one.

Grendel's mother, a monster-wife, a she-devil, mourned over her misery. She was doomed to dwell in dread waters, in cold-flowing currents, after Cain had slain his only brother, his father's son, by the sword. Then did God brand Cain with the mark of the murderer and banish him from the joys of mankind, to wander forever in the wilderness. Thence, from Cain's loins, sprang forth a spawn of accursed fiends. Grendel, warring and hateful, was one of those. At Heorot, the fiend found a warrior watchful, waiting for war. There the monster grappled with Beowulf. But Beowulf was mindful of the glorious gift God had bestowed upon him in the strength of his grip, and he trusted in the Almighty to assist him, succor him and support him. And thus he overcame the foe, humbled the fiend from Hell. Grendel then, feeling shame, departed, this enemy of mankind, deprived of contentment, to seek out his Death-dwelling. And his mother now, ravenous and bloody-minded, purposed to set out upon that mournful mission, the Death of her son to avenge.

She came then to Heorot, wherein the Danes slept throughout the hall. Soon there was a return of sorrow unto the nobles when Grendel's mother burst her way in. The dread was the less, even as much as is the strength of a woman warrior, the war-horror of a female, compared with that of men, when the hammer-hardened blade with its sharp edge, streaked in blood, shears through the boar-symbol upon the enemy's helmet.

Then in the hall was the hard-edged sword drawn. Many a broad shield was lifted firm in hand. No one thought of helmet or chain-mail when terror laid hold of him.

In haste now was Grendel's mother. She wished to be gone from thence, to save her life when she was espied. Swiftly the she-demon seized one of the nobles in a tight grasp, and then fled unto her fen-lair. This nobleman, whom the accursed she-devil had slain in his bed, was for Hrothgar the dearest of his heroes, his most beloved comrade between the two seas, a mighty shield-warrior, renowned for his bravery.

Beowulf was not there. Another abode had been appointed unto the glorious Geat, after the giving of treasures. Uproar filled the hall of Heorot. Grendel's mother had carried off the famed gore-bestained claw of her son. Then was grief renewed unto the Danes in their dwellings. That was no good bargain, when those on both sides must barter with the life-days of their friends.

Then was Hrothgar, the aged ruler, the grey-haired war-thane, woeful in spirit when he came to know that his long-trusted liegeman had lost his life, his dearest companion dead. Unto Hrothgar's chamber was Beowulf, dauntless victor, brought in haste. As day was dawning, Beowulf and his warriors, noble champions all, hied themselves to where the wise King awaited, wondering whether God Almighty would ever turn this tide of troubles. The war-worthy hero strode across the floor-boards with his followers. The hall-timbers resounded. Beowulf stepped forward to address Hrothgar. He inquired of the King if he had passed a peaceful night.

XX

Hrothgar, protector of the Danes, spoke:

"Ask not about peaceful. Grief is returned unto the Danish folk. Dead is Aeschere, Yrmenlaf's elder brother, and my trusted friend and counselor. He stood beside me in battle when warriors clashed and swords clanged. Such should every soldier be, steadfast and stalwart, as Aeschere was. Now a wandering death-ghost has slaughtered him in Heorot with her hands. I know not whither that cruel creature has fled, rejoicing in her kill. She has taken vengeance for the fight of yesternight, wherein you did slay Grendel with a mighty grip in a merciless manner, because he did for so long ravage and kill my kinsmen. He fell in fight, with forfeit of life. Now comes another evil fiend, to seek revenge for her son, and she has performed a deed of exceeding blood-vengeance that shows her hatred unyielding. Thus it seems to many a thane who mourns that treasure-bestower with heavy heart-sorrow. Now does the hand lie lifeless, which was once each wish so willing to fulfill.

"I have heard the inhabitants of this region, my people, relate that such a pair they have sometimes perceived, huge marsh-stalkers from another world, the moor-lands wandering. One of these, as far as they could affirm with greatest certainty, was in the likeness of a woman. The other wretched creature trod the tracks of exile in the image of a man, save that he was bigger than any man. In days of yore, those who dwell upon Earth have named him Grendel. These miserable creatures know of no father. Neither do they know of any such benighted brood begotten before them. They frequent the inaccessible places, the lair of the wolf, the wind-whipped cliffs, the fearful fen deeps, where flows the stream downward beneath dark crags to underground waters. It is not farther from hence than the distance of a mile where the lake stands. Over it, the frost-bound boughs hang, firmly rooted in the black soil, casting bleak shadows over the water. There, each night, appears a fearsome sight—a fire upon the flood. There lives not, among the sons of men, one so wise who can fathom the bottom thereof. Nay, even the great-antlered stag, driven fleeing from afar, harried by hounds, would rather yield up his life upon the bank than plunge into its waters. That is not a good place. Thence ascends a surge of shadowy waves unto the clouds when the winds bestir evil storms, till the air is defiled and Heaven weeps.

"Now, once more, help must come from you alone. You know not yet the lair of that sin-laden creature, the perilous place wherein she abides.

Seek it if you dare. I shall reward you with ancient treasures, with coiled gold, for waging this warfare, as formerly I did, if you return victorious."

XXI

Beowulf, son of Ecgtheow, spoke:
"Sorrow not, wise one. Better it is that a man avenge his friend than that he mourn overmuch. Each of us must await the end-day of his Earthly existence. Let him who can, attain glory ere Death. When his days are told, renown is the warrior's worthiest reward. Arise, Guardian of the Realm. Let us away at once, the trail of Grendel's Dam to seek. I promise you she shall not find refuge, neither deep in the embrace of the Earth, nor in mountainous forests, nor in the depths of the ocean, wherever she will wander. This day, endure with patience every woe, as I expect you will."

Then leaped onto his feet the old man. He rendered thanks unto God, the Almighty One, for Beowulf's brave words. A war-horse was then fitted with bridle and saddle for Hrothgar, a courser with a braided mane. The wise King rode forth, stately and splendid. The foot-troop of shield-bearers marched behind their Lord. Making their way over the woodlands, they clearly beheld the tracks of the she-demon as she trod unto the murky moor, bearing away with her the body of the best of thanes, bereft of life, who, with Hrothgar, ruled the realm. Then Hrothgar, the son of Princes, proceeded over steep stone cliffs, along unfamiliar narrow passes, upon precipitous promontories above the abodes of many a water-monster. Onward he fared, with a few warriors who knew the land, to explore the terrain until, of a sudden, he discovered mountain trees hanging over massive grey rocks, a woeful woods. The lake below was blood-bestained and bubbling. Then were the Danes anguished at heart, for many a hero 'twas hard to bear, when, on the cliff above the water, they came upon the head of Aeschere.

The waves boiled with blood, with burning gore. The troopers gazed upon the waters. Anon the horn sounded its fervent battle-song again and again. The warriors seated themselves to take their rest. They beheld then all manner of sea-creatures, writhing snakes, strange sea-dragons swimming in the deep, water-monsters lying upon the rocky headlands, serpents and unruly water-beasts, such as those which surface at dawn to sink some sorrowful ship. Upon hearing the noise of the battle-horn's blast, the creatures hastened away, bitter and enraged. Beowulf, with an arrow from his bow-string, separated one of the creatures from its life, from its struggle with the waves, when the keen war-shaft pierced unto its vitals. The creature seemed to swim slower when Death was upon it. Speedily was the strange wave-dweller sorely hard-pressed by the Danes' barbed boar-spears, beset by hostile attacks and pulled onto the promontory. The men looked upon the terrible beast with disgust and loathing.

Then did Beowulf don his martial mail, not fearful of Death. His sturdy chain-mail shirt, hand-hammered, brightly-hued, must soon the wave depths explore. Well could it ward the warrior's body, should a malevolent hand attempt to hurt his heart or break his breast-bone. His head was guarded by Hrothgar's gleaming helmet, which would dare the deeps of the flood and wend its way through the eddies. The helmet was richly emblazoned, encircled with an iron guard wrought by a weapon-smith in seasons long past, wondrously worked, set round with boar-images, so that never would sword-blade brandished in battle bite into it.

And this helmet was not the least of helpful objects, which, in that time of need, Hrothgar's orator, Unferth, loaned unto Beowulf. He also gave the redoubtable Geat a hilted sword named Hrunting. This renowned blade was the most formidable among ancient weapons. Its edge was iron, etched with patterns of poison, tempered in battle-blood. Never had it failed any hero who hefted it with his hands in combat against his foes upon the field of battle. This was not the first time the famed sword was destined to accomplish a dauntless deed.

When he lent the weapon unto the better warrior, in sooth, Unferth, son of Ecglaf, sturdy in strength, remembered not the words he had, wine-drunk, erstwhile spoken. He, himself, dared not venture his life, perform noble deeds of valor 'neath the tossing of the waves. So Ecglaf forfeited fame and his repute for honor. But this was not so with Beowulf, after he had clad himself for battle.

XXII

Beowulf, son of Ecgtheow, spoke:

"Let you, famous son of Healfdene, wise Prince, gold-friend of warriors, now that I am ready to sally forth on this venture, bethink yourself of what we spoke about a while since. You affirmed that if, in your cause, I should lay down my life, you would evermore serve me in the stead of a father, when my Earth-days were done. Be you a guardian to this group of thanes, my warrior comrades, if I fall in combat. The goodly gifts you bestowed upon me, beloved Hrothgar, I beseech you to send unto my King Hygelac. Then may the Lord of the Geats, son of Hrethel, perceive, when he gazes upon that treasure of gold, that I encountered a generous ring-giver and enjoyed the good of his company while I could. And let Unferth, far-famed noble, have my precious heirloom, this battle-sword splendid, this hard-edged weapon. With Hrunting, Hrothgar's renowned war-blade, to aid me, shall I seek glory, or else Death will carry me off."

With these words, Beowulf hastened away and plunged into the lake. He would in no wise wait for an answer. The surge of the wave currents covered the warrior. Almost a day's length elapsed before he could behold the bottom thereof.

Soon did she, who, for a hundred winters, had haunted the domain of these waters, grim and greedy, ravenous for gore, discover that some one of men from above was come to explore this dwelling-place of demons. The she-devil grabbed Beowulf. She seized him in her foul claws. But she could not harm him. His body was unscathed. His chain-mail shielded him. Through his war-shirt, the hateful monster could not thrust her hostile claws. Then did the sea-wolf, when she reached the lake-floor, bear the Prince of rings unto her lair. Whereupon, Beowulf, no matter how redoubtable he might be, strove in vain to wield his weapon.

A host of sea-monsters set upon him in the deep. Many a sea-beast assailed his battle-shirt with tusks and teeth. They harried the hero. Then the warrior perceived that he was now in some infernal grotto, where the shallow waters could work him no harm. Nor, on account of the height of the cavern, could the sudden clutch of the current catch him. He saw fire-light, a gleaming blaze shining bright.

Then Beowulf espied the accursed she-demon of the depths, the fearsome sea-witch. He swung his war-sword with all his strength. The ring-adorned blade sang a brutal battle-song upon her head. But the visitor discovered that the battle-blade would not bite, would not end the she-beast's life. Its hard edge failed the Prince of heroes in his time of need. This renowned sword had known, in times past, many a hand-to-hand strife. Often had it sheared through helmet and armor of an ill-fated warrior. It was the first time that ever this excellent treasure-sword had failed its glory to fulfill.

Once again was Beowulf resolute, mindful of heroic deeds. His courage was not a whit diminished. The wrathful warrior cast down his sword. The inlaid blade, sturdily-wrought and steel-edged, lay upon the ground. In his own strength he now trusted, in his own mighty hand-grip. Thus must a man do when he intends to gain unending glory in battle. He cared not for his life.

Then did the Prince of the War-Geats seize Grendel's mother fast by the shoulder. To him the struggle was not unpleasing. Inflamed by rage, he flung his deadly foe unto the ground. She swiftly gave him requital with the grim grip of her claws and grappled with him.

The strongest of warriors, the best of foot-soldiers, was then weary with wrestling. He stumbled and fell. Then did the she-beast hurl herself upon the fallen warrior. She wielded her war-knife, broad and bright-edged. She would wreak vengeance for the murder of her son, her only offspring. But, upon his shoulder, lay the woven chain-mail. That protected his life 'gainst the blade, withstood the entry of point and edge thereof. Beowulf, son of Ecgtheow, champion of the Geats, would have perished under the wide waters, had not his sturdy chain-mail armor afforded him help. And had Most Holy God not brought about victory in battle. Once Beowulf had regained his footing, the Omniscient Lord, Ruler of Heaven, arranged for Justice to prevail.

XXIII

Then Beowulf beheld, amidst the war-gear, an ancient blade blessed with victory, forged by ogres. The sword was the glory of warriors, its edges undaunted. This blade was the choicest of weapons. But it was larger and heavier than any man, other than Beowulf, might wield in battle. The weapon was good and glorious, wrought by giants.

The champion of the Geats, wrathful and battle-grim, grasped the sword-hilt with both hands. Despairing of life, he wheeled about and smote the she-demon upon her neck. That blow broke her neck-bone. The blade sliced through her body. Foredoomed, the she-monster sank upon the ground. The blade was bloody. The hero rejoiced in his triumph.

Then blazed forth light. 'Twas bright within the cavern, as when, from the sky, there shines Heaven's torch brilliant. Beowulf looked about his surroundings, then walked alongside the cave wall, raging and resolute. He held the weapon high, hard by the hilt, seeking Grendel. Beowulf wished to repay the monster for the many onslaughts he had wrought against the Danes. For the times the foul fiend had slain Hrothgar's hearth-subjects in their sleep, devoured fifteen men of the Danish folk whilst they slumbered, and bore away as many more. That was an unspeakable outrage.

But, now, the valiant victor espied the lifeless body of Grendel, war-torn, lying upon the ground, victim of the battle at Heorot. The corpse moved one last time, when Beowulf, with a savage sword-stroke, severed Grendel's head from his body.

Soon thereafter, the sage counselors who awaited with Hrothgar the issue of the conflict saw, upon the deep, the surging waves all a'troubled, the sea blood-bestained. Whereupon, the aged men, grey-haired, spoke together of the great warrior, and said they expected not Beowulf to return. They expected not to see again that noble Prince, exulting in conquest, appear before the renowned King Hrothgar. To many it seemed that the accursed sea-wolf had slain him.

The ninth hour of the day was arrived. It was then that the intrepid Danes forsook the headlands. Homeward wended the gold-friend of men, Hrothgar. But the Geats remained there, heart-sick, regarding the waves of the water. They wished for the event, but despaired of beholding their comrade and Lord once more.

It was then that the death-dealing sword of Beowulf began, because of bitter blood-gore, to melt as icicles in Spring. 'Twas a wondrous marvel to behold, like unto ice when the Eternal Father, He who has dominion over Time and Tide, loosens the fetters of frost and unchains the ice-floes. That is the true God.

Beowulf, Prince of the Geats, took naught of treasure-wealth from that cavern, though he perceived much therein. He carried away only Grendel's head and the hilt of the giants' bejeweled sword. The wave-patterned blade of that sword was earlier melted away, made molten by the boiling blood of Grendel's mother. The blood of that strange she-demon who perished there was so poisonous.

Soon was Beowulf swimming unto the surface, he who had in war triumphed over the battle-fall of his foes. He swam upward through the waters. The wave-surges were all cleansed, the mighty depths were purified, now that the hateful she-fiend had given up her life-days and this uncertain world. Swimming with an undaunted heart, the defender of sea-farers came unto land then. He took pride in his sea-booty, the great prize he bore with him to the surface.

The excellent troop of thanes advanced to greet their leader. They rendered thanks unto God. They rejoiced in their Prince, that to see him safe and sound was vouchsafed unto them. The hardy one's helmet and breast-plate were speedily loosened. Now did the lake lie still. The waters beneath the Heavens were bestained by the blood of battle.

Forth then did the Geat warriors fare. Merry and mirthful, they returned along the way they had come unto that place. The men, bold as Kings, carried Grendel's head from the sea-cliff. That head was too heavy for two of the stout-hearted warriors to bear. It took four of the Geats, with toil, to convey the monster's head upon a stake unto the gold-hall. So, presently, to the high hall did the fourteen fearless Geats, battle-brave, come. With them came their leader, proud among men, striding unto the mead-hall. Then did Beowulf, bold in exploits, renowned in glory, courageous hero of the conflict, enter the hall to address King Hrothgar. And then, onto the hall floor, where the Danes sat drinking, was Grendel's head dragged by the hair. It was a horror for the warriors and the Queen to behold. That was a wondrous sight. They all stared upon it with astonishment.

XXIV

Beowulf, son of Ecgtheow, spoke:

"Lo! Hrothgar, son of Healfdene, Prince of the Danes, we have joyfully brought unto you this sea-booty which you now behold, as a token of triumph. With great difficulty did I escape with mine life in that war beneath the waters. The battle was all but ended, had not the Almighty defended me. I failed to accomplish aught with Hrunting in that fight, though that weapon was worthy. But the Ruler of Men gave me to espy, upon the wall, in splendor hanging, a huge ancient sword—oft has He helped those who are friendless—so that I might wield the weapon. Then, in that struggle, when the occasion was given unto me, I smote the she-demon who dwelt in that den. Whereupon, that battle-sword with the wave-patterned blade melted away, burned up as the boiling blood spurted out, the hottest of battle-gore. I bore the hilt away from your enemies.

"I have avenged, as was fitting, the evil done unto the Danes, the massacre of your folk. Now I do vow unto you that, henceforth, you may slumber in Heorot free from care. You and your band of warriors and all the thanes among your people, old and young, no longer need dread mortal injury from that threat, as ere you did, O Prince of the Danes."

And then was that golden hilt, the ancient product of giants, given unto the hands of the old warrior, the hoary chieftain. That handiwork of wondrous smiths, after the fall of the demons, had passed into the keeping of Hrothgar, Prince of the Danes. After the hostile-hearted fiend Grendel, the enemy of God, and his mother, had abandoned this life, it came unto the power of the best of world-Kings between the two seas, of those who lavished gifts in the North-Lands.

Hrothgar spoke. He beheld the hilt of the old heirloom. Upon it was inscribed the origin of that ancient strife 'twixt Good and Evil, when the Great Flood, the raging waters, drowned the race of giants. Their Fate was fearful. That race was alienated from the Eternal Lord. The Almighty God, thereupon, gave them final requital for that in the surge of the seas. Upon the golden hilt was verily graven, set down and inscribed in runic letters, for whom that sword, the best of blades, with twisted hilt and carved serpents, had first been wrought.

Then spoke the wise one, Hrothgar, son of Healfdene. All were silent.

"Hark. He who upholds Truth and Righteousness among the people, this old protector of the homeland who remembers all that has befallen, affirms that this Prince of the Geats, Beowulf, was born the better man. Your glory shall be exalted in every land, both far and wide, Beowulf, my friend. You hold all steadfast, prudent and resolute. I will fulfill my promise of friendship toward you, as before we agreed. Now, must you be a great solace unto your people, a support unto your own warriors, for many long years.

"Be not as King Heremod was in former times. He grew not to grace the Danish folk, but, instead, to bring grievous destruction and direful death-woes upon them. Filled with wrathful rage, he slew his own table-companions, his dear comrades, until he, that haughty Prince, knew not the joys of men. Though Almighty God had endowed him with might and the delights of power, and had uplifted him high above all men, yet within his bosom there dwelt a blood-fierce spirit. Unto the Danes, as he should have done according to custom, he gave none of ring-treasures. And, thus, bereft of happiness, he suffered finally from that endless hostility toward his people.

"Learn you from this lesson. Grasp virtue tightly unto your breast. To you have I recited this tale so that you may accept the wisdom of my many winters. 'Tis wonder to relate how Almighty God, in His generosity of spirit, does bestow, upon mankind, understanding, chattels and honor. He has dominion over all things. At times, He suffers the heart of a high-born man to achieve its desire. God grants him the joys of domain over his commonwealth, the stronghold of men to keep. The Lord makes the nations of the Earth subject unto him, an ample kingdom. In his folly, he believes all this will never come to an end. He lives amidst luxury. Nothing afflicts him, neither illness nor age. Nor does sorrow darken his spirit. Nor does hostile strife from any state show sword-hatred. All the world does turn at his will. He knows not the worst that may befall.

XXV

"Until, within him, overweening pride and arrogance awakens and burgeons. Then does that guardian, his conscience, the sentry of his soul, slumber. Its sleep is too deep, with cares encompassed. Unannounced, the slayer draws very near unto him. Armed with bow and arrow, the assailant aims with malice. Then he, who knows not how to defend himself, is hit in the breast with the sharp-toothed missile. He is stricken by the foul, evil mandates of the Devil. All that he had so long held dear now does seem unto him to be paltry and valueless. He covets fiercely. No gold rings does he give unto his people with generous pride. Because of the greatness that God, the Wielder of Glory, had erstwhile bestowed upon him, he forgets and flouts the future that Fate has ordained for him. Yet, in the end, it comes to pass, as it must to all men, that the transitory flesh fails and falls doomed. Whereupon, another King appears who joyously distributes the treasures, the old acquisitions of the warrior, without thinking on his predecessor.

"Defend yourself from such baleful thoughts, beloved Beowulf, best of warriors, and choose for yourself the better path—everlasting honor. Be not overly proud, renowned hero. Now, for but a little while, lasts the fullness of your life-vigor. Soon shall illness or sword-edge separate you from strength. Or else, it will be the embrace of the flames, or the surge of the seas, or the assault of the blade, or the flight of the spear. Or old age with its attendant horrors. Or it may be that the gleam which brightens your eye will fade into darkness. 'Twill happen early, noble warrior, that Death shall subdue you.

"Thus have I ruled over the Danes for half a hundred years. I defended them with spear and sword against many tribes who would wage war upon us. I reckoned with no adversary under the wide expanse of Heaven. Lo, then, a reverse came unto me in mine own land, grief after joy, when Grendel, that Hellish foe, became my constant invader. I suffered heart-heavy sorrow from those ruthless raids. Thanks be unto God, Eternal Lord, that, after long-lived tribulations, I may, at last, behold that blood-bestained head. Go now unto your bench, Beowulf, illustrious in battle, and enjoy of the banquet. When morrow dawns, you shall have a wealth of treasure."

Beowulf, the Geat, was glad at heart. He went straightaway to take his seat, as the prudent Prince bade him. Then was again, as before, a feast agreeably set before those warriors, renowned for courage, who sat in the hall. The veil of night cast darkness over the noble heroes.

Then did the company all arise. The grey-haired King, the aged Dane, would visit his bed. And it pleased Beowulf, the Geat, sturdy shield-warrior, to take his rest. Forthwith did a servant, who, by custom, ministered to the needs of a thane, as a seagoing warrior was wont to have in those days, lead Beowulf unto his chamber. He was weary from his exploit and far from his home.

The stout-hearted man slumbered. The high hall towered above, wide-gabled and gold-gleaming. The guest slept within, till the black raven sang of the rapture of Heaven. Then was come thither the bright sun shining, hastening away the shadows. The warriors quickly arose from their beds. They were ready to return homeward unto their people. Beowulf, bold sojourner, wished to sail his ship far from thence.

Then stalwart Beowulf ordered that Hrunting, brave battle-sword, be borne unto Unferth, son of Ecglaf, and commanded him to take the sword, that excellent iron. Beowulf rendered him thanks for the loan thereof and said he accounted it a good friend in battle. He chided not the edge of that blade. That was a gallant warrior.

Eager for their departure, the Geats stood ready in war-trappings. Beowulf, their Prince, advanced unto the throne where Hrothgar sat. Whereupon, the hero, undaunted in combat, greeted King Hrothgar.

XXVI

Beowulf, son of Ecgtheow, spoke:

"Now we seafarers, come from afar, wish to say that we would fain return unto our King Hygelac. You have welcomed us well and kindly feted us. Gracious was your greeting. If I may gain greater affection from you, O ruler of heroes, through war-like deeds, than those I have already accomplished, I shall ever be ready to aid you. Should I hear, over the compass of the seas, that your neighbors threaten you with acts of war, as those who hate you have done before, I shall carry a thousand thanes hither, a host of heroes to help you. I know that Hygelac, Lord of the Geats, protector of the people, though he is young in years, will assist me, both with words and works, to defend you well. Then will I journey hence to honor you with my lance, the support of my strength, when you have need of men.

"If then Hrethric, your son, should betake himself unto the court of the Geats, therein will he find a multitude of friends. No man who visits distant nations is more welcomed there than a valiant and noble hero."

Hrothgar spoke to answer him:

"All-Knowing God has sent these words unto you. Never have I heard so youthful a man speak so wisely. You are powerful in might, prudent in mind and sage in speech. If it comes to pass that the spear, grim war, sickness or steel should carry off your King Hygelac, defender of the country, and you yet hold fast to life, then I verily believe the Geats will find no worthier man to be King and treasure-guardian of heroes, if you should wish to rule the kingdom of your kinsmen. Your spirit likes me better, the more I know you, beloved Beowulf. You have caused a common peace to ensue between our peoples, the Geats and the Danes. From murderous strife and cruel conflict, such as once they waged, shall they now refrain. For as long as I reign over this realm, so wide-spread, our treasures will be shared. Many a man shall greet another, over the sea-bird's bath, with excellent gifts. The ring-prowed ship shall bear our offerings and love-tokens over the seas. I know your clan respect the ancient traditions and are, in every way, blameless, and they are, moreover, steadfast toward both friend and foe."

Then Hrothgar, son of Healfdene, defender of warriors, gave unto Beowulf, in the hall, treasures twelve. He bade Beowulf return safely to his well-beloved people with these offerings, and come back again, ere long. Then did the Prince of the Danes, a King great in his nobility, kiss Beowulf, best of thanes, and embrace him about the neck. The grey-haired man wept sorrowful tears. Hrothgar was old and wise. He knew there was but faint chance he would behold Beowulf's countenance again, and meet this brave man in council once more. Beowulf was so dear unto the aged King that he could not restrain the emotions that welled within his breast. Though the Geat was not his kinsman, a blood-bond burned in his heart toward the beloved warrior.

Thence did Beowulf, the warrior glorious with gold, exulting in treasure, stride over the grassy plain. His sea-going vessel, riding at anchor, awaited its master. As the Geat warriors hastened onward, Hrothgar's liberality they lauded at length. He was a peerless King, in every way unflawed, till old age, which spares no man, stole his strength.

XXVII

Now the troop of Geat warriors, young and brave, wearing their war-shirts of interlocked chain-mail, came unto the shore. The trusty coast-warden espied the warriors approach, as erstwhile he did. This time, from the height of the hill, he greeted the guests not with hostile words, but galloped down the hillside to meet them. He proclaimed that these soldiers in shiny armor, descending unto their ship, would receive a joyous welcome home from their Geat countrymen. Upon the sand, the broad-bosomed craft with curved prow was laden with armor, steeds and treasures. The mast towered above Hrothgar's hoard of riches.

Beowulf gave unto the guardian, who had kept watch over their ship, a sword, bound with gold, so that this Dane was thereafter more highly esteemed at the mead-bench, as the possessor of that ancient blade.

Then the vessel left the land of the Danes and plowed through the deep water. A sea-cloth was set firm unto the mast, a sail made fast with taut ropes. The ocean-borne timbers creaked. Not then did the wind o'er the billows hinder the wave-floater from its journey. The sea-traveler sped ahead, its foaming neck furrowed forth over the waves. The ring-prowed ship sailed over the streams of the seas till the sailors sighted the cliffs of their Geat homeland, the well-known promontories.

Driven by the wind, the ship ran ashore upon the strand. The harbor-watchman, who had long gazed out upon these waters awaiting his beloved comrades, hastened unto them. He bound the broad-bosomed craft fast unto the shore with anchor-bonds, lest the force of the ocean waves carry away that winsome vessel. Then Beowulf commanded that the treasure of Princes, the ornaments and beaten gold, be carried ashore. They would not have to travel far from thence to seek the treasure-giver, King Hygelac, son of Hrethel, where he dwelt with his comrades, near unto the sea-cliff.

Stately was the building wherein the King, most renowned, lived. It was a high and exalted hall. Within that hall also dwelt Hygelac's wife, Hygd, daughter of Haereth. She was young, wise and high-minded. Few were the winters she had abided in that stronghold. She was not haughty, not niggardly in gifts of precious treasure unto the race of Geats. She was not like Thryth, imperious Queen, who was prideful, an unforgivable sin. No bold man among the beloved comrades, save only her father, dared venture to gaze upon her face. If one such did, perchance, look upon Thryth, his Fate was sealed with death-bonds. The unfortunate wretch would be bound with hard-twisted fetters. Brief would be the interval after they did seize him. Soon, the edge of the sword would speak, and the blade would render judgment. It was a violent death. That is not a fit custom for a Lady to practice, though she be a peerless Queen. The Queen who is a Weaver of Peace should not deprive a dear subject of his life-days because of a fancied wrong.

But the companions of Hemming, kinsman of Offa, would, in no wise, allow this. Over their ale-benches, the drinkers related another tale. They said that Thryth, once she was given in marriage unto King Offa, young war-champion, she wrought less mischief and fewer acts of malice. At her father's bidding, Thryth, gold-adorned, sailed over the ocean-flood to the palace of Offa. Afterwards, she graced well the throne and was famed for her virtue. She enjoyed, in her life-time, the good that Fate had ordained for her. High love she held for her husband, that greatest of heroes. He was, as I have heard tell, the best King of the sons of Earth which the two seas do encompass. Hence, Offa, spear-bold soldier, was widely praised for his gifts and his victories. He ruled his realm with wisdom. From him sprang his son, Eomer, guardian of heroes, grandson of Garmund, kinsman of Hemming, mighty in battle.

XXVIII

Then Beowulf, the bold one, and his band of warriors strode along the shore, the wide sandy beach. The world's candle shone upon them, the sun bright from the South. They hastened on their way unto the place where, they learned, the worthy young battle-King, Hygelac, slayer of Ongentheow, was bestowing rings in the stronghold. To Hygelac was Beowulf's arrival speedily reported. He was told that Beowulf, defender of warriors, Hygelac's shield-comrade, was come alive unto the palace, unscathed from the play of war. With haste in the hall, as the King had commanded, a space was cleared for the soldiers.

After Beowulf, he who had survived the mortal struggle, addressed solemn words of ritual greeting unto his faithful King, he seated himself before his Monarch, kinsman facing kinsman. Queen Hygd, daughter of Haereth, passed throughout the hall, bearing mead-cups. The thanes were dear to her. She carried flacons of mead for the hands of the heroes.

Hygelac began then to fairly ply his comrade with questions in that high hall. He sorely longed to learn of the exploits of the Sea-Geats.

Unto Beowulf spoke Hygelac:

"How fared you upon your journey, worthy Beowulf, when, on a sudden, you determined to seek out strife afar over the salt-water, a battle at Heorot? Have you bettered somewhat the widely-known woes of Hrothgar, that renowned Prince? As my heart grieved, I brooded over this venture of yours, my beloved liegeman, with deepest disquiet. For a long while, I besought you not to wage war against that murderous monster. Suffer the Danes, I entreated you, to settle their struggle with Grendel themselves. I now utter thanks unto God that, safe and sound, I once again behold you."

Beowulf, son of Ecgtheow, spoke:

"Hygelac, my Lord, my battle with Grendel is widely renowned among the sons of men. People speak of the grim struggle between Grendel and me in that very place wherein the demon wrought evils unending upon the Danes. All that I avenged. Thus none of Grendel's kin on Earth, not even a one who lives longest of that loathsome race, embraced by sin and deceit, may boast of that midnight fight.

"At first I came thither unto the great ring-hall to greet Hrothgar. Soon did the noble son of Healfdene, when he came to know my intention, give me a seat beside his own sons. The troop was joyous. In all my life-days never beheld I such mirthful men savoring mead more 'neath the vault of Heaven. From time to time, Wealhtheow, Hrothgar's high-born Queen, peace-pledge between nations, passed through the lofty hall, heartening the young warriors. She oft proffered a gold ring-band unto a hero ere she went to her seat. And, at times, the daughter of Hrothgar bore the ale-cup to the veterans, each in turn. I heard the men seated in the hall call her Freawaru, when she bestowed gilded treasures upon the heroes.

"She, young and adorned with gold, is betrothed unto Ingeld, gracious son of Froda. Her faith has been plighted by Hrothgar, her father, protector of the kingdom. He counts it wise his daughter to wed to the Heathobard Prince, and, by so doing, to end the deadly feud between the Danes and the Heathobards. But seldom, when a Prince is slain, does rest the avenging spear, even though the bride be fair.

XXIX

"It will please him not, Ingeld, Prince of the Heathobards, and his band of thanes when he enters into the hall with his bride, Freawaru, daughter of Hrothgar, and perceives that the noble sons of Danes are therein splendidly feasting. The Danes will be wearing their spoils of battle, the gleaming armor of the Heathobards' ancestors, and bearing hard-edged and ring-adorned swords, weapons that once Ingeld's forebears wielded in the clash of shields, until their lives and those of their dear comrades they lost in combat against the Danes.

"Then, over his ale-cup, an aged Heathobard spear-warrior, who espies these ancient heirlooms in the hands of his enemies and who recalls the slaughter of his men by thrust of sword—grim is his heart—will speak aloud. He, sad in spirit, will begin to turn the temper of his young leader toward thoughts of war-hatred.

"These words will the old warrior utter:

" 'Are you not able, my friend, to recognize the sword, that precious steel, which, into the fray, your father carried in his final fight. Beneath his war-mask, your father fought valiantly till the bold Danes gained mastery of the battle-field and, after the down-fall of heroes, slew him. Now, here, some son of these murderers strides in this hall, exulting in the treasure, boasting of the blood-shedding and wearing the armor which you should rightfully hold in possession.'

"And so, upon every occasion, does the old warrior admonish and provoke with bitter words till, at last, the season comes that a thane of Freawaru will slumber forever, blood-bestained, after the bite of the blade, his life forfeit on account of the deeds of her father. Thence does the slayer escape with his life. He knows the land well. And, thus, is broken on both sides, the solemn oaths of nobles. After, deadly rancor will well up in the heart of Ingeld. His wife-love will cool from his anguish of mind. Wherefore, I count not upon the good feelings of the Heathobards, that their pact of peace with the Danes will be without treachery, or their friendship fast.

"But, now, will I continue to speak of Grendel, so that you, bestower of treasure, may well know the issue of that hand-to-hand combat of heroes. After the Jewel of Heaven had fled over the far fields, the demon came raging, the dreaded night-foe, to seek us out where, steadfast in spirit, we stood sentry over the hall. There was the battle mortal for our companion Hondscio. His fall was fated. He was the first to perish, that war-girded champion. Grendel devoured my noble kindred thane. He swallowed up the whole body of that beloved man. Yet the bloody-toothed beast, bent on malice, did not wish to go forth from that gold-hall with empty hands. Renowned for his might, he pitted himself against me, and laid hold of me with fervent grip. A huge pouch hung by his side, wide and wondrous, strongly worked with artfully-wrought bands. It was made, with the Devil's devices, from the skin of dragons. The fiendish foe, that savage source of evil deeds, would fain thrust me therein, though free of sin was I. But he could not do so, when I, wrathful, did stand upright.

" 'Twere too long to relate how I repaid that scourge of the people for his every evil deed. 'Twas there, my Prince, that I did bring honor unto your kinsmen by my labors. The demon fled from Heorot. For a short space did he yet live. However, his right hand he left in Heorot. He, abject and heart-sick, went from there discomfited and sank unto the depths of the lake.

XXX

"When daylight dawned and we all at the banquet-table sat, Hrothgar, King of the Danes, paid me for that deadly struggle with plates of gold, and with manifold treasures. There was singing and merriment. The aged Dane, who had heard many stories, told tales of days of yore. At times, the battle-brave King would pluck the joyful string, the sweet-sounding harp. He would recite stories, veracious and mournful. Or the great-hearted King would relate legends of wonder. And then the old warrior, troubled with years, would bewail his lost youth, his prowess in combat. His heart welled within him when he, wise with many winters, recalled to memory a multitude of deeds.

"Thus did we take our pleasure there all that day, till another night came unto men. Anon was Grendel's mother full ready to wreak vengeance. She set out upon her doleful journey. Dead was her son, killed by the war-wrath of the Geats. The monstrous woman avenged her child. In her fury, she murdered a warrior. There did the life depart from Aeschere, wise aged counselor. Nor, when morning was come, could the war-weary men of the Danes consign their comrade unto the flames. They could not lay their beloved liegeman upon the funeral pyre. The dreadful she-demon had carried off his body in a deadly embrace beneath the mountain-torrents. For Hrothgar, that was the heaviest of burdens which had long befallen the leader of the people.

"Then did the King, sad in spirit, entreat me, for your sake, to hazard my life under the surge of the waves. He beseeched me to seek glory with deeds of valor. Much reward did he promise unto me. I found then, as is well-known, that she-devil, the savage guardian of the sea-floor. We grappled there hand-to-hand. The waters ran red with blood. I hacked off the head of Grendel's mother with a hardy blade in that briny hall. Scarce did I escape with my life. I was not yet doomed to die. Then did Hrothgar, son of Healfdene, protector of warriors, endow upon me, once again, many a treasure.

XXXI

"Thus, seemly did the King of the Danes live. I wanted for naught in gain as recompense for my might. Hrothgar, son of Healfdene, gave unto me manifold treasures of mine own choosing. These gifts will I now gladly proffer unto you, noble King of warriors. All my advantages derive from your Grace. I have but few kinsmen, save for you, King Hygelac."

Then Beowulf bade his men bear unto him the boar-image banner, the excellent battle-helmet, the iron-grey armor and the splendid war-sword.

Beowulf spoke:

"Hrothgar, that wise Prince, gave into my hand this war-gear. He told me to relate unto you the whole of its history. He said that his elder brother, King Heorogar, Prince of the Danes, owned it for the space of a long time. Yet he wished not to bequeath it unto his son, bold Heoroweard, though he was faithful to him. Use well all these treasures."

I heard that there followed soon thereafter four swift steeds, apple-yellow, all alike. Arms and horses did Beowulf then present unto King Hygelac. So ought a kinsman to act. He should not weave a web of wiles with deep-hid craftiness, nor devise the death of a dear comrade. Beowulf, nephew to Hygelac, steadfast in battle, was most loyal unto him. Each was mindful of the other's well-being. Then I heard that Beowulf bestowed upon Hygd, Hygelac's Queen, the necklace, wondrous treasure, which Wealhtheow, Hrothgar's wife, had given him. He gave her also a trio of steeds, strong and saddle-bright. Resplendent shone that necklace upon Hygd's breast.

Thus did Beowulf, renowned in battle, celebrated for mighty deeds, manifest his valor and act with honor. Never did he slay his hearth-companions in drunken rage. His heart was not cruel. Courageous in combat, greatest in strength of heroes then living, he guarded with care the glorious gift which God gave him. Yet, when but a youth, Beowulf had long been despised by the sons of the Geats. They accounted him as worthless. Nor would the Lord of the liegemen grant him honor at the mead-bench. They fully believed him to be indolent, a weak Prince. But, unto the warrior blessed with glory, came requital for all the unkind slights he had suffered in earlier days.

Then Hygelac, defender of warriors, the King mighty in battle, ordered the sword of Hrethel, gold-bedecked, to be brought unto him. No Geat ever knew of a statelier treasure in the shape of a sword. Hygelac laid

that sword in Beowulf's lap, and bestowed upon him seven thousand
measures of land and a hall and the throne of a Prince. Common to both was
land in that realm, estates inherited by natural right. However, unto the King
was greater dominion granted in consequence of his reign.

It thereafter befell, in the clash of conflict, that Hygelac was slain. In
later days, the war-Swedes, bold battle-heroes, sought out Heardred, son of
Hygelac, amidst his valiant comrades upon the field of combat and assailed
him with battle-blades and killed him. The shelter of Heardred's shield
availed him not.

Into Beowulf's hand then did come the rule of this broad realm. Well
did he reign over it for the space of fifty winters. He was a wise King, an
aged guardian of the land. But, then, a Dragon began to rampage during the
dark of night. This beast kept watch over a treasure-hoard in a high stone
burial-barrow. Beneath it lay a passage, unknown to mortals. Some man
entered therein and drew near unto the heathen hoard. His hand grasped a
large goblet, adorned with jewels. The thief stole away with this treasure and
fled, whilst the Dragon slept. The Dragon was wrathful. All the sons of the
Geats came to know the rage of the Dragon.

XXXII

That thief did not despoil the Dragon's hoard willfully, nor meant he
to endanger his life. In great distress, he, the slave of some hero's son, fled
in fear from hostile blows and sought shelter. The slave, a sinful man, found
refuge within that death-barrow. At the fearsome sight, the man took fright.
Terror seized him. Dread of the Dragon overcame him. But, before the
wretch escaped, he seized that precious bejeweled vessel and hastened away
with it.

There was a multitude of ancient treasure in that earth-house,
carefully secreted there, in days of yore, by the last survivor of an illustrious
lineage. It was the immeasurable legacy of a noble race. Death had carried
them all off in earlier times. One, alone, he who lived there longest, was left
alive, the last of the clan. He bewailed his kinsmen. He foresaw a like Fate
for himself. He knew that but for a brief interval would he enjoy the long-
gathered treasure.

The burial-barrow, newly-ready, stood upon the open plain near unto the sea-waves, hard by the headland. Entry into it was secure. Then that last Guardian of the Rings laid within it a hoard of golden treasure so great that its equal would be hard to find.

Few words spoke he:

"Hold you, O Earth, this wealth of warriors, now that heroes can no longer. Lo, it was from you that valiant men did erstwhile wrest it. War-death, fierce combat, has ravished the lives of every man of my people. They have witnessed the last of pleasures in the mead-hall. There is none who may wield the sword, none who may burnish the golden chalice, precious drinking vessel. My company of veteran warriors is departed. Now must the hardy helmet, adorned with gold, molder in this tomb. Now slumber forever the polishers who should scour the battle-mask. And the chain-mail, which endured stroke of sword upon shattered shield, rots with the warrior who wore it. None of this battle-gear will travel to distant lands with our War-Lord beside his heroes. There is no joy in the music of the harp, no rapture of the timbrel. Nor does an excellent hawk swoop through the hall. The swift stallion does not stamp its hooves in the court-yard. Grievous is the destruction that the plague of war has visited upon mankind."

Thus, sad in spirit, did the sole survivor lament his sorrow. By day and by night, he mourned, till the foul billows of Death overwhelmed his heart.

And then that ancient twilight-stalker, the Dragon who flies by night, encompassed by fire, found the precious treasure unguarded. This wicked beast seeks out barrows. Those who dwell upon Earth greatly dread the Fire-Dragon. Its wont is to hunt for a hoard under the ground where, over the span of many ages, it guards pagan gold, though this profits not the creature.

For three hundred winters did that scourge of the people keep watch over that mighty treasure-house beneath the ground, till a certain man aroused choler in its breast. The slave carried unto his master the golden goblet and begged him for forgiveness. Thus was the hoard discovered and the treasure taken from thence. The wretched slave was granted his wish. His master beheld that magnificent ancient work of men for the first time.

Then awakened the Dragon. For the Geats, sorrow and woe began anew. The Dragon, ruthless by nature, crawled along the rock-face. The beast discovered the foot-track of the thief. With stealthy craftiness had he stepped unharmed past the head of the sleeping Dragon. Thus may a man not doomed to die, by the grace of God, easily escape evil and misfortune.

The guardian of the gold-hoard fervently sought the intruder. The Dragon wanted to find the man who had wronged it while it slept. Flaming forth fire and fierce of mood, the beast circled and circled again the exterior of the mound. There was no man to be seen in that wasteland. But the Dragon rejoiced in the thought of battle, was eager for war-like work. Then it returned unto the barrow in search of the precious cup. It soon perceived that some man had plundered the gold, stolen the precious treasure.

The Dragon abided, impatient, till evening arrived. The guardian of the barrow was wrathful in spirit. That hateful creature was determined to avenge with fiery breath the theft of the dear-valued drinking-vessel.

Then was the day departed, to the delight of the Dragon. No longer would it remain upon the mound. The Dragon flew forth, enfolded in fire. It was a fearful beginning for the sons of the soil. And, swiftly thereafter, the Fate of their ruler, Beowulf, treasure-giver, would come to a grievous ending.

XXXIII

Then did the Dragon begin to discharge great fearsome flames to burn happy houses. The blazes shot high, bringing terror unto men of the land. No being would that loathsome creature leave alive as it flew through the air. Far and near, the devastation, the cruel hostile hatred, wrought by the Dragon was clearly visible. The onslaught of that belligerent ravager harried and persecuted the people of the Geats.

Ere dawn of day, the Dragon hied back to its well-hidden hoard. It had encompassed with furious fire the land-dwellers, with flames and with burning. The Dragon trusted in the safety of the barrow, in the ramparts and bulwarks, and in its own war-strength. But the Dragon was deceived.

To Beowulf then was the truth of the terror speedily made known. His own home, best of buildings, treasure-throne of the Geats, was destroyed by waves of fire. That brought sorrow unto the spirit of the great man. He felt grief in his heart. Beowulf, wise man, believed he had angered Almighty God, the Eternal Lord, by breaking some ancient commandment. His breast boiled within him, troubled by black thoughts. This was not his custom.

The Fire-Dragon had completely destroyed, with flaming breath, the stronghold of the people, washed by the waves. So therefore, Beowulf, the War-King, Prince of the Geats, planned vengeance upon the creature for that. Then did the defender of warriors, the leader of heroes, command to be wrought for him a splendid war-shield, made all of iron. He knew full well that wood from the forest would avail him not, linden wood against fire-flame. Thus would this noble ruler meet the end of his life-days, the conclusion of his time upon Earth, and the Dragon along with him, though it had long guarded the treasure-hoard.

The Prince of Rings disdained to challenge the air-borne beast with a band of warriors, with a mighty host. He feared not the fight. He made little account of the Dragon's war-power, valor and prowess, for he had survived many onslaughts. Defying danger, he had, in clash of combat, a hero blessed with triumph, purged Hrothgar's high hall and slain both Grendel and his Dam, of that loathsome race.

And that was not the most arduous of contests in which Beowulf fought. He partook of the war in which Hygelac, King of the Geats, benevolent Prince of the people, was killed in the campaign against the Frisians. Hygelac, son of Hrethel, perished by blow of blood-thirsty blade in the Netherlands. Whereupon, Beowulf, by dint of his own strength, escaped from that field of strife by swimming over the sea. Beowulf carried with him the battle-armor of thirty warriors as he swam through the waves. His adversaries had no cause to exult in that warfare, when they wielded linden-wood shields against him. Few would emerge, unscathed, from an encounter with that battle-hero, to seek their homes.

Then did Beowulf, son of Ecgtheow, solitary swimmer, over the expanse of oceans, return unto his people. And there did Queen Hygd, widow of Hygelac, tender unto Beowulf treasure and kingdom, rings and throne. She trusted not in her son, Heardred, that he could defend the crown of the homeland against hostile hordes, now that King Hygelac was dead.

But the stricken nation succeeded not in persuading Beowulf to become master over Heardred, or to agree to rule the realm. However, Beowulf upheld Heardred among the people with helpful counsel, graciously with honor, until Heardred came of age and ruled the Geats.

And then, from across the seas, came Swedish exiles, sons of Ohthere, seeking refuge. They had risen up against Onela, defender of the Swedes, their renowned Prince, best of Sea-Kings, generous bestower of rings. That marked the end of King Heardred. Onela descended upon the Geats with a mighty army. For the shelter he rendered unto the rebels, Heardred received a mortal wound from blow of blade. And, after Heardred had fallen, did Onela return unto his homeland. He left Beowulf to ascend unto the Princely throne and rule over the Geats. That was a good King.

XXXIV

And it came to pass, thereafter, that Beowulf was mindful of requiting the fall of his Prince. He befriended and aided the wretched Eadgils, one of the exiles from Sweden. Whereupon Eadgils sailed o'er the wide sea with warriors and weapons. He waged warfare and wreaked cold vengeance. King Onela's life he took.

Thus did Beowulf, son of Ecgtheow, emerge uninjured from every conflict, every dangerous assault, every deed of daring, until that day was come when he was Fated to fight the Dragon. With comrades eleven, the Lord of the Geats, swollen with rage, went to behold the Fire-Dragon. He knew, by then, whence the feud arose, what had caused the murder of his clansmen. The precious vessel had come into his possession from the hand of the one who had found it. That slave, he who had brought about the beginning of the strife, became the thirteenth member of that band of heroes. The slave, dismayed and shamed, was compelled to lead the way unto the Dragon's den. Against his will, he guided the men to that burial-mound. It lay beneath the ground, near unto the surge of the waters, the wrath of the waves. Within, it was full of jewels and gold, manifold treasures untold. The monstrous guardian, war-like, grown old in its lair, waited there, warding the hoard. No easy possession would it be for any man to gain.

And then the King, Beowulf, brave in battle, seated himself on the headland. The gold-bestower of the Geats wished Good Fortune unto his hearth-companions. His soul was sad, troubled, brooding upon Death. Fate was too nigh. It would soon greet the old man, seek the treasure of his soul, sunder life from his body. Not much longer would the spirit of the Prince be enveloped in flesh.

Beowulf, son of Ecgtheow, spoke:

"In my youth-days I survived many war-onslaughts, many times of conflict. I remember all that. I was seven winters of age when King Hrethel, guardian of treasure, friendly ruler of the people, from the hands of my father took me. King Hrethel kept me and cared for me. Treasure he bestowed upon me, and banquet. He bore in mind our kinship. Never, while I there abided, was I less dear unto him than any of his sons, Herebeald and Haethcyn, or mine own Hygelac. For the eldest, Herebeald, was spread a bed of untimely death. By unlucky chance did Haethcyn, his brother, hit him with an arrow from his horn-bow. He missed his mark and struck his kinsman, one brother the other with the bloody shaft. That was a death which could not be avenged. It was a dreadful transgression, weighing sorely upon a weary heart. But, notwithstanding, the young Prince must needs part from life with vengeance untaken.

"So is it mournful for a grey-haired man to live to see his young son swing from the gallows. Then must he chant a chronicle of woe, sing a song of sorrow, as his child hangs there, food for the ravens, whilst he, aged and bent with years, is unable to render him help. And ever will he be reminded, each morning, of his boy's departure. He cares not to await the birth of another heir in his household, after the first has felt Death's doleful sting. Forlorn, he gazes upon his son's dwelling, a wasted wine-hall, a resting-place for the winds. It is a home bereft of all joy. The horsemen slumber, the heroes in their graves. There is no music of the harp. There is no merriment in the court, as once erstwhile there was.

XXXV

"Then does the old man retire unto his chamber, there to chant a lay of grief for what he has lost. Too wide and empty to him is the land and the homestead. Thus did Hrethel, defender of the Geats, feel sorrow welling in his heart for his son, Herebeald. He could, in no way, take vengeance upon the slayer for that murderous deed so foul. Nor could he hurt his son with hostile acts, though he loved him not. And then, sick with the sorrow which had befallen him, he forsook the joys of men and chose the light of God. When from life he departed, he left unto his sons land and stronghold, as a rich man is wont to do.

"And it came to pass then, after Hrethel had perished, that there was strife and struggle between Swedes and Geats. Over the wide water, there was bitter grievance, hostile malice of warriors. The offspring of Ongentheow were resolute and relentless. They wished not to pursue a pact of peace. They contrived cruel massacre and merciless ambush at Hroesnabeorh. But, as is widely known, mine own kinsmen avenged that dispute and offense, though at a dear cost, for one man paid with his life.

Unto Haethcyn, King of the Geats, did that war prove fatal. Then I heard
that, in the morrow, Hygelac sought revenge upon his brother's killer,
Ongentheow, with the edge of his blade. But Eofor, Hygelac's thane, did
find the Swedish King first. Whereupon, Eofor sheared his enemy's war-
mask in twain with his sword and cleft open his skull. The aged Swede fell,
pale and mortally stricken. The Geat hero's hand forgot not that feud. Eofor
did not withhold the death-blow.

"For all the treasures which King Hygelac bestowed upon me, I repaid
him with my shining sword in combat, as Fortune was pleased to permit me.
Hygelac gave me land, homestead and the joy of an ancestral seat. He had
no need to seek lesser soldiers, to buy with treasure, weaker warriors from
amongst the Germans, the Spear-Danes or the Swedes to fill his ranks. Ever
did I fight alone in the vanguard of the order of battle. So shall I wage
warfare all my life-days, while this sword endures, that, late and early, has
served me so well.

"I slew Daeghrefn, champion of the Franks, with mine own hand in
the presence of the veterans of both armies. He was unable to convey the
precious breast ornament of Queen Wealhtheow unto the Frisian King.
Daeghrefn, the standard-bearer, fell in that battle. He was a brave Prince.
Daeghrefn was not slain by my sword-edge. My war-grip broke his bone-
cage and stilled the swell of his heart. And now must the edge of this sword,
my hand and hard blade, fight for the Dragon's treasure-hoard."

Again Beowulf spoke, uttering boastful words for the last time:

"I braved many battles in my youth-days. Today am I the aged
protector of my people. I shall now seek the struggle to achieve glory, if that
hateful despoiler will emerge from his earth-hall to fight me."

Then Beowulf bid farewell unto each of his men, brave helmet-
bearers, beloved comrades:

"No blade would I wield, no weapon against the Dragon, if I knew
how else to accomplish my word-boast, how to grapple with the beast, as
erstwhile against Grendel I did. From this beast do I expect hot war-fire and
blast of venomous breath. Therefore I bear shield and chain-mail shirt. I will
not yield the space of a footstep before the guardian of the barrow. We will
fight at the rampart and Fate, which rules over every man, shall decree the
outcome. I am undaunted, so I forebear all vaunting words against the
winged enemy.

"Await me by the barrow, you warriors in armor, you heroes in battle-
gear, to see which of us twain will better survive his wounds after the deadly
clash of combat. This struggle is not yours, nor is it meet for any but me
alone to measure might 'gainst this monster, to accomplish valorous deeds.

With courage shall I gain that gold, or else the battle, direful death strife,
will carry off your King."

Then did the famous warrior arise beside his shield, brave beneath his
helmet. In battle-mail went he beneath the steep-rising rocky cliffs. He
trusted in the strength of a single man. That is not the path of a coward. Soon
Beowulf, stalwart hero, who had survived much turmoil of battle when
troops clashed, did perceive an arch of stone standing in the wall. From
thence a stream flowed forth from the barrow. The surge of that spring was
flaming with war-fire. By reason of the Dragon-Flame, he could not long
endure the heat of the passage near unto the hoard without being burned. So
fierce was his fury that the Prince of the Geats let fly a roar from his breast.
The stout-hearted man shouted out a battle-cry. His challenge resounded
through the grey-stone cavern.

Hate was aroused. The guardian of the treasure-hoard heard the sound
of a man. Too late was it now for proffer of peace. Then issued forth from
the rock the Dragon's flaming breath, fiery war-fumes. The Earth thundered.
Beowulf, Prince of the Geats, lifted his shield against the loathsome enemy.
The heart of the coiled Dragon sought strife. The valiant War-King drew his
sword, that ancient heirloom, its edges sharp. Both of them, Hero and
Dragon, bent upon destruction, felt fear of the foe. Undaunted, Beowulf,
ruler of his people, stood behind his tall shield. The Dragon coiled and
uncoiled itself. Clad in his battle-armor, Beowulf awaited the onslaught.

Now did the Dragon, breathing fire, come slithering out, hastening
unto its Fate. His shield protected life and limb of the renowned Prince for a
shorter space of time than he desired. For the first instance ever, Fate denied
Beowulf triumph in battle. The Lord of the Geats brandished his sword and
struck the scaly beast with his precious blade. The blade bit the bone, but
weakened and gave way. Its bite was less formidable than Beowulf needed,
hard-pressed by adversity.

Then was the guardian of the treasure-hoard enraged by that battle-
blow. It spewed forth baleful fire. The war-flames spread wide and far.
Beowulf, gold-friend of the Geats, could boast of no glorious victory. His
naked battle-blade, that iron of trusted worth, had failed him, as it should not
have done. 'Twas no easy task for the son of Ecgtheow to forsake this
Earthly-plain forever. Against his will he must needs dwell in some other
domain, as each man must do when the days loaned unto him become due.

Soon then did the fearsome foes clash again. The guardian of the
hoard was heartened anew. The Dragon's breath flung forth searing flames.
Beowulf was ringed round with fire. He who had erstwhile ruled a nation
endured great agony.

By no means did Beowulf's comrades, sons of Princes, stand to his defense with valor in combat. They turned in fear and fled into the woods, seeking safety. But the soul of one man was tormented with distress. In one who means well, nothing can set aside the love of a kinsman.

XXXVI

That man was called Wiglaf, son of Weohstan, much beloved shield-warrior. He was a Prince of the Danes and kin to Aelfhere, the Swede. Wiglaf now witnessed Beowulf, his Liege Lord, suffering oppressive heat under his helmet. He called to mind the bounty Beowulf had bestowed upon his family, the rich homestead of Weohstan, his father, and vast property-rights. Wiglaf could not hold back. His hand seized his shield, yellow linden-wood. He unsheathed his ancient sword, known to warriors as once belonging to Eanmund, son of Ohthere, King of Sweden. In warfare, with the edge of his sword, had Weohstan slain Eanmund, friendless exile, when from Sweden he fled. Then Weohstan carried unto Eanmund's uncle, King Onela, the shining war-mask, ringed chain-mail and ancient sword made by giants. But Onela gave Weohstan all that, his kinsman's battle-gear, ready war-trappings. Onela spoke not of the feud, though his brother's son had been felled.

For many winters did Weohstan keep the war-gear, sword and chain-mail, till his son was ready to display daring as erstwhile his father had done. And then, amidst a conclave of Geats, he gave unto his son, Wiglaf, that goodly array of battle-gear, whereupon, aged in years, Weohstan departed this life and set out upon his journey hence.

Now, for the first time, the young warrior was to withstand the clash of combat beside his noble Lord. His spirit was undaunted. The ancestral blade of his kinsman failed not in the fray. This the Dragon discovered after they met in battle.

Mournful of mind, Wiglaf spoke, uttering many fitting words unto his comrades:

"I recall the time we drank mead in the hall and pledged to be ever faithful unto our Liege Lord. We promised our ring-giver that we would requite him for the war-gear, helmets and sharp swords, he bestowed upon us, if need such as this should befall him. Wherefore, he selected us from all his army for this venture. He believed us worthy of glory. He esteemed us to be the best spear-warriors, the boldest helmet-fighters.

"Our King, protector of the people, for our sake, intended this audacious act to accomplish alone, because, among men, he has achieved the most splendid successes, the most daring deeds. Yet now it is the day when our Liege Lord requires the strength of valiant warriors. Come. Let us go unto him. Let us succor our War-Prince while the flames rage, fierce dreaded fire-fight. As for mine own self, God knows I would fain have the flames embrace my body together with my treasure-bestower. Methinks it is unseemly for us to carry our shields homeward, lest first we fell the foe and defend the life of the Prince of the Geats. Well do I know that, by his valorous exploits, he does not deserve to suffer affliction alone, to fall unaided in conflict. For us both shall sword and helmet, shield and battle-mail, serve to fight together."

Then went Wiglaf boldly through the Dragon's deadly billows. He bore his battle-helmet and his war-gear to the assistance of his Lord.

Wiglaf spoke but few words:

"Beloved Beowulf, carry on bravely. In your youthful years of yore, you affirmed that, while life should last, you would in no wise allow your glory to be diminished. Now, undaunted hero, renowned for valorous deeds, you must defend your life with all your strength. I will stand by your side to aid you."

After these words, the Dragon came raging once more. That fearful malignant beast, flashing with waves of fire, rushed forth to seek its foes, the hated men. The edges of Wiglaf's shield burned from the blazing breath of the Dragon. His war-armor availed not the young spear-fighter. But Wiglaf, steadfast, sought shelter behind Beowulf's shield when his own was burnt by the flames.

Then the Warrior-King was again mindful of glory. Beowulf, driven by anger, with his war-sword, smote the Dragon's head with all his force. But Naegling, the hero's ancient battle-blade, broke asunder. His sword failed him in the fight. It was not ordained unto Beowulf that edges of iron would help him in combat. His hand was too strong. 'Twas said that his might tried beyond its endurance every blade, even one tempered by blood. That sword aided him naught.

For the third time, that despoiler of men, the malevolent Fire-Dragon, renewed its assault. The beast assailed the bold hero. Battle-grim and burning with rage, the Dragon bit deep into Beowulf's neck with its sharp fangs. Beowulf's body was bathed by his life-blood. His body-gore welled out in waves.

XXXVII

As it is said, then did Wiglaf, perceiving the dire need of his King, display courage, strength and daring, for this was his nature. He paid no mind to the Dragon's fiery head. Though his hand was burned, Wiglaf, warrior in armor, to help his kinsman, struck the hateful creature in its nether parts. His sword, bright and burnished, sank into the beast's underbelly. The Dragon's fire began to diminish.

Then did Beowulf come to his wits. He brandished the dagger, keen and battle-sharp, which he wore upon his breastplate. The defender of the Geats sliced the Dragon's midmost part open. They had felled the foe. Their courage had driven out its life-force. They had slain the beast together, noble kinsmen. So should a man be, a friend in time of danger.

For Beowulf, that would be his last triumph. It was to be the end of his great works in the world. Then did the envenomed wound, which the Fire-Dragon had inflicted upon him, begin to scald and swell. He soon found that the fatal poison boiled in his breast. Aware of his Fate, the doomed Prince stepped forward to sit before the rampart. He gazed at the giant structure, saw how the long-lasting earth-works were upheld by sturdy pillars and arches of stone.

Whereupon, Wiglaf, most excellent thane, with his hands, bathed with water the wounds of his beloved Prince, blood-stained and war-weary, and unbound his helmet.

Beowulf spoke. Despite his injuries, the wound that was fatal, he would fain utter some words. Full well he knew that he had finally spent his allotted time of Earthly bliss. All the measure of his life-days had been counted. Death was exceeding near.

"I would have liked to give unto a son of mine this war-gear, if it had been granted unto me to have an heir of this my body and my blood. But no son have I. For the space of fifty winters did I reign over this nation. No King of the nearby clans did dare attack me with armies in battle, nor try me with terror. At home I bided steadfastly what Fate might bring, guarded well my portion, feuds I fomented not, nor swore ever an unjust oath. Now, stricken with mortal wounds, I am consoled by all this. When the life-force passes from my body, the Almighty Ruler of Men will have no reason to charge me with the sinful killing of kinsmen.

"Now, beloved Wiglaf, hasten to behold that precious hoard beneath the grey stones, now that the Dragon lies dead, asleep forever from grievous wounds, bereft of its treasure. Go quickly, that I may gaze upon the ancient riches, the gold-wealth and gleaming jewels. By so doing, will I be more easily able to yield up my life and my people, whom I have ruled for so long."

XXXVIII

Then heard I that Wiglaf, son of Weohstan, after this speech of Beowulf, did speedily obey his battle-wounded Lord. He entered into the barrow, wearing his shirt of chain-mail and brandishing his sword. Exulting in triumph, the bold young thane beheld a vast store of shining jewels and glistening gold upon the ground. On the walls of the ancient night-stalker's lair, he perceived wondrous works. He saw goblets therein, drinking vessels of men from times past, dull and unburnished. There was many a helmet, old and rusted, and a multitude of arm-bracelets artfully made. Such a wealth of gold, buried deep in the ground, may swiftly overwhelm any mortal with overweening pride, let him hide it who will.

And Wiglaf espied then a banner woven all of gold hanging high above the hoard. It was the greatest of wonders, cunningly crafted by skilled hands. So bright was its radiance that the intrepid warrior was able to see the ground and behold the treasure. No vestige of the Dragon was there. The sharp edge of the sword had put an end to the creature.

Then, it is said, Wiglaf plundered the hoard-treasure, that ancient work of giants. He burdened his bosom with as many cups and plates of gold as he desired. He took also the golden flag, brightest of banners.

The sword-blade of Beowulf, aged King—its edge was iron—had deeply injured the Dragon, long-lived guardian of the golden hoard. Its fire-breath, in midnight rampages, had issued forth flames of fear to protect the precious treasure, till violently was the beast slain.

And then did Wiglaf, in all haste, laden with treasures, make to return unto his Sovereign. Anxiety afflicted him. Wiglaf, brave of heart, worried whether he would find Beowulf, Prince of the Geats, though sorely wounded, still drawing breath, in the place wherein he had before left him. Bearing these treasures, the young thane found Beowulf, renowned Prince, his beloved Liege Lord, with blood flowing, at his life's end. Once again did he lave his Lord with water, till words began to issue forth from Beowulf's breast-hoard.

Beowulf, aged hero in extremis, spoke. He gazed upon the gold.

"I render thanks, with expressions of devotion, unto the Ruler of all Mankind, the King of Glory, the Lord Everlasting, for these treasures which I here behold, that I have been able to gain such valuables for my people before Death overtook me. I have bartered my life-days for this booty. Now must you, Wiglaf, henceforth, attend well to the needs of my subjects. No longer can I tarry here.

"Bid you my renowned war-thanes to construct them a fine burial-mound high upon the headland beside the sea, after the flames of my funeral pyre have turned to ashes. It will tower over Hronesness as a memorial to my nation, so that sea-farers, when they sail their ships from afar o'er the mists of the darkening flood, shall afterwards call it Beowulf's barrow."

Then did the valorous King take from his neck the collar of gold and give it unto Wiglaf, young spear-warrior. He gave him also his gold-adorned helmet, his gold ring and chain-mail shirt, and bade his thane use them well.

Beowulf spoke:

"You are the final remnant of our race, of the Waegmundings. Fate has carried off all my kinsmen, fearless warriors, to their destiny. I must needs follow them."

That was the last word from the aged Prince, the final thought from his heart. He would now taste the hot war-flames of the funeral fire. From his bosom departed his soul to seek the glory of the just.

XXXIX

Then was the youthful warrior greatly grieved to behold, upon the ground, his most beloved King, at the end of his life-days. It was a sorrowful sight. The fearsome Fire-Dragon, slayer of Beowulf, likewise lay dead, deprived of life, vanquished by violence. No longer would the coiled Dragon rule the ring-hoard. For hard edges of iron, battle-notched swords, forged by hammers, had ended its time upon Earth. The fiery sky-flier, stilled by its wounds, fell to the ground, hard by the treasure-house. It would fly no more, flaming gloriously through the night sky, proud of its precious prizes. The Dragon lay, unmoving, upon the ground because of the War-Prince's handiwork.

Few were the men, so I have heard, no matter how strong and steadfast they might be, who had the courage to brave the fiery breath of the venomous beast. Indeed, few were the men who were fearless enough to steal into the ring-hall, intending to plunder its treasure, lest the guardian thereof be awake and watching his cache. Beowulf had paid for these lordly riches with the price of his Death. Both Beowulf and the Dragon had reached the end of this fleeting life.

Erelong, those who had fled the battle forsook the woods. Their number was ten, faithless thanes, who feared to flourish their spears at the hour of their King's great distress. With shame, they bore their shields and war-gear unto where the aged warrior lay dead. They gazed upon Wiglaf. Wearied, the war-soldier sat at the side of his Lord, vainly trying to wake him with water. In no whit was Wiglaf able to; it availed him not. Much as he desired it, he could not rouse the breath of life in his Sovereign. He could not overturn the will of God. The judgment of the Almighty would determine the destiny of every man, as it always has and always shall.

And then, from the young warrior, swiftly came a grim reproach to those who, erstwhile, had lost their nerve. Wiglaf, son of Weohstan, spoke. Heartsick, he looked upon the unloved men.

"Lo! It is requisite for one who would speak the truth to say that your Liege Lord bestowed treasures upon you and, yea, even the armor in which you now stand. Beowulf, Prince to his thanes, would oft give helmets and mail-shirts to you men seated on benches in the mead-hall, the most excellent war-gear he might find anywhere, far or near. But, when battle beset him, these arms were wasted on warriors who deserted him. Beowulf, King of his people, could boast not of the valor of his comrades at arms. However God, Who decrees victories, granted him, when bravery was needed, the strength to avenge himself unaided with the edge of his sword. I could render him little assistance in the struggle to save his life, but I attempted to aid our kinsman beyond my measure. The deadly Dragon's might waned when I smote it with my sword. The fire flamed less fiercely from out of its mouth.

"Too few were the protectors who thronged around our Prince when the time of peril was upon him. Now shall bestowing of riches and giving of swords, pleasures of landholdings and joys of home, come to an end for your race. When Kings from afar should learn of your cowardly flight, infamous act, every man of your people will be condemned to wander the Earth, bereaved of all rights to landed possessions. To every warrior is death preferable to dishonor."

XL

Then did Wiglaf command that the outcome of the battle be proclaimed unto the band of Geat warriors waiting high upon the sea-cliff. The troop of warriors, shield-bearers, sat sad at heart all that morning. They were in doubt as to the issue of the fight. They wondered if their beloved King would return or if this day would be the end of his life-time. The herald who rode to the headland held back but little of the news. He spoke verily unto all present who heard him.

"Now is he, who graciously grants gifts unto our people, Lord of the Geats, laid upon his death-bed. From the assaults of the deadly fire-breather, he sleeps on the slaughter-bed. By his side lies the Dragon, that slayer of men, stricken with knife-wounds. With his sword Beowulf could, by no means, inflict harm upon the beast. Wiglaf, son of Weohstan, sits by the side of Beowulf, the living warrior beside the lifeless one. Weary at heart, he maintains vigil over friend and foe.

"Now may the people expect a waging of warfare. Soon shall the Franks and the Frisians come to know of the fall of our King. The fearsome feud against the Franks was begun when King Hygelac sailed with his fleet of sea-borne soldiers down the Rhine. His foes vanquished him in combat. With overwhelming numbers, they defeated the chainmail-clad warrior and forced him to yield. Hygelac was slain in battle. He died amidst his troops. No longer would our Chieftain give treasure unto his valiant comrades. For us, ever since, has there been a state of war with the Franks.

"Nor do I expect aught of peace or amity from the men of Sweden. It is widely known that their aged King Ongentheow slew Haethcyn, son of Hrethel, near unto Ravenswood, when the men of the Geats, in their arrogance and vainglorious pride, attacked the warlike Swedes. Soon did sage Ongentheow, old and terrible, give an answering blow in requital. He killed Haethcyn, the Sea-King, our leader, and rescued his own abducted Queen and consort, mother of Onela and Ohthere, although she had been plundered of her gold. And then did he pursue his mortal foes who fled before him until, sore beset, they entered into Ravenswood, bereft of their Lord.

"Then, with a mighty army did Ongentheow besiege the Geats in the forest, weary and wounded, who had escaped his swords. Oft times, through the night, woe he taunted unto that wretched remainder. Said he that, in the morrow, he would hack them into pieces with the edge of his sword. And some would he hang on the gallows-tree as sport for the birds.

"But rescue came with dawn of day to these woebegone warriors. They heard the battle-cry of Hygelac, his war-horn and trumpet. Their valorous champion had followed them and rallied his stalwart soldiers to their defense.

XLI

"The bloody swath cut by Swedes and Geats, deadly onslaught of soldiers, was everywhere perceived. The feud of folk against folk was aroused. Then did the aged King, Ongentheow, sorrowing overmuch, retreat with his kinsmen to seek his stronghold. He and his warriors withdrew to higher ground. Of Hygelac's battle-skill and prowess in combat he had heard. He desired not to challenge the sea-voyagers. He could not defend his riches, his wife and his children against the assault of the raiders from across the deep. Thus, did he carry himself and his people unto the earth-rampart.

"And then did the Geats pursue the fleeing Swedes. Hygelac's battle-banners advanced proudly across the plains. The Geat warriors broke through the earth-walls of the enclosure. It was then that hoary-haired Ongentheow was brought to bay by edge of sword. He was forced to submit to the judgment of Eofor alone. Whereupon, Wulf, brother of Eofor, with his weapon, struck the skull of the Swedish King in anger. Ongentheow's blood flowed forth from beneath his hair. But the aged Swede felt no fear. He swiftly turned and repaid the mortal blow with an even more powerful strike. However, brave Wulf could not return the blow unto the old man. Ongentheow had stove in Wulf's helmet, hewn it in twain, so that, stained with blood, he slowly sank to the ground. But Wulf was not yet fated to die. He recovered from his hurt, although the wound was deep.

"When his brother fell, Eofor, thane of Hygelac, smote Ongentheow with his broad blade, ancient sword wrought by giants. The sword broke through the Swede's shield-wall and stuck in his huge helmet. Then was the King fallen. The protector of the Swedish people was dead.

"Then, when the field of battle was won, many were the Geats who rushed to bind up the wounds of Wulf and helped him to arise. Whereupon, the warrior Eofor despoiled the dead warrior Ongentheow of his war-gear. He took his iron-mail shirt, hard-hilted sword and helmet also. Unto Hygelac did he carry these spoils of war. The King accepted the gift and graciously promised him rewards among the men in the mead-hall. And he did fulfill his promise thus: when he again came unto his homeland, Hygelac, Lord of the Geats, son of Hrethel, did bestow upon Eofor and Wulf, for that war-assault, exceeding wealth of treasure. He granted unto each of them vast landholdings and linked rings of gold. No man on Earth could reproach this King for his generosity. Eofor and Wulf had achieved glory in combat. And then, unto Eofor, did Hygelac give his only daughter, pride of his home, as an earnest of good faith.

"Such is the feud and the hostility, deadly enmity of men, which I believe will befall when the Swedes shall learn that our leader lifeless lies. In earlier days did Beowulf defend our treasure and kingdom 'gainst those who abhorred us and would assail us. After the fall of heroes, he did further the common good and accomplish more and more of hero-deeds.

"Now is haste most fitting that we should behold our people's King, and convey him, who bestowed rings upon us, unto the funeral pyre. Boundless treasure of gold untold shall melt away with the bold one, dearly purchased. In the end, Beowulf bought these rings with his blood. The flames shall devour them. The fire shall envelop them. No warrior will wear a treasure-ornament in remembrance. No maiden fair will wear an adornment about her neck. Wretched in spirit, bereft of gold, shall they henceforth tread upon foreign soil, exiled and banished, for the space of many winters, now that our leader of liegemen has forsaken forever laughter, revels and joyous song. Many a spear, morning-cold, will be raised with fist, hefted aloft by hand. The dulcet sounds of the harp shall not wake these warriors. Instead, the caw of the death-black raven, eager to eat the doomed, shall speak of many things, shall relate unto the eagle how it, with the wolf, consumed the carcasses of the slain."

Thus did the dauntless messenger deliver the grim tidings. He was not much mistaken in his prophesies or his words. And then all the war-troop arose. Woeful and weeping, they betook themselves unto Eagles' Cape to gaze on the astounding sight. There they saw, lying upon the sand, their beloved Beowulf in his final resting-bed, he who had once given them rings. The last of days was come to the great man. Beowulf, War-King, Prince of the Geats, had met a glorious Death.

But, first, they beheld the Fire-Dragon, wondrous creature. The hateful beast lay upon the ground before them. The many-hued Dragon, grim terror, was scorched with flames. The measure of it was full fifty feet from head to tail. It had, in former times, rejoiced in flying through the air of a night and then gliding down unto its den. But, now, Death's grip held it fast. No longer would it enjoy Earth-caves.

By the side of the Dragon were strewn beakers and vessels, dishes and precious swords, rusted and eaten away, as if they had rested there for a thousand winters within the Earth's embrace. That great bequest, gold of an ancient race, was guarded by an enchantment. No man was permitted to touch the ring-hoard unless God Himself, True King of Triumphs—He is the Protector of Heroes—should grant it unto one whom He desired to lay open the treasure, to such a mortal as seemed fitting unto Him.

XLII

It was then observed that the path profited him little who had wrongfully plundered the hoard, wealth hidden beneath the wall. The guardian thereof, despicable Fire-Dragon, had slain Beowulf, a warrior like unto no other. Then was the feud angrily avenged. It is not possible to know when a warrior, a hero above heroes, will meet the end of his destined days, when he will no longer sit at the mead-bench with his kinsmen. Thus was it with Beowulf when he sought out the guardian of the barrow in perilous battle. He, himself, knew not how his leaving of life would befall.

The great Princes, who had buried the treasure therein, had cast upon it a curse till doomsday, that whosoever might pillage the gold would be guilty of transgressions. That man would be interred in heathen shrines, held fast in Hell-bonds, punished with plagues. But Beowulf knew not of the owner's evil spell over the treasure, riches of gold.

Wiglaf, son of Weohstan, spoke:

"Oft has a nation come to know grief because of the actions of one man. Such has now happened unto us. We could not prevail upon our beloved Prince, protector of the Kingdom, to heed our counsel not to draw near the guardian of the gold. We entreated him to let the beast lie where long it had lain, to live in its lair till the end of the world. But Beowulf would not yield. He pursued his noble destiny.

"The treasure-hoard, grievously gotten, has been beheld. Too unkind was the Fate which carried our King to that place. I was therein and gazed upon the manifold riches in that death-barrow, once I could enter into it. By no means was that journey beneath the earth-wall a pleasant one. Swiftly I seized a weighty burden of treasure-hoard and bore it hither unto my King. He was yet alive and clear of mind. The aged man, in his anguish, spoke many words. He commanded me to greet you and bade you memorialize the deeds of your friend by raising, upon this site of his funeral pyre, a lofty barrow, high and glorious. Of men, near and far, o'er the whole world, while he was still possessed of wealth and stronghold, was he the worthiest warrior.

"Let us now hasten and see once more that store of precious jewels, that wondrous sight beneath the wall. I shall guide you and take you thereunto, that you may gaze upon rings a-plenty and gold in abundance. And let the bier be made ready, speedily prepared, so that, when we come forth, we may bear our Lord, beloved Beowulf, unto the place where he shall abide forever in the Almighty's keeping."

Then did Wiglaf, son of Weohstan, battle-brave hero, give orders unto rich thanes, holders of homesteads, leaders of the people, to gather fire-wood for the funeral-pyre upon which the good man would lie.

Wiglaf, son of Weohstan, spoke:

"Now shall the fire consume this leader of warriors. The dusky flames will devour him, who oft endured the storm of iron-showers, when arrows shot from bow-strings, shafts of fletched barbs, struck the shield-wall."

And now the wise son of Weohstan did summon forth seven of the King's thanes. They were the best and most noble. Wiglaf was the eighth battle-warrior who entered with them beneath the enemy's roof. The warrior who walked before them bore, in his hand, a light-blazing torch. No lots did they cast for plundering this hoard when they beheld the treasure in the barrow, without a guardian, lying there abandoned. And little did they scruple that they should swiftly carry the precious treasure forth from out of the cavern.

And then did they hurl the Dragon, deadly demon, over the cliff-side, for the waves to take. The surge of the flood swallowed the guardian of the treasure. Then was wound gold laid upon a wagon, a countless multitude of riches. Upon that wagon was also placed the Prince, grey-haired warrior, and his body was borne unto Whale's Ness.

XLIII

For Beowulf then did the people of the Geats make ready, upon the promontory, a funeral-pyre heaped high for the burning. Upon it they hung helmets, battle-shields and bright-shining breastplates, as their King had wished. Whereupon, the weeping warriors laid down their far-famed Prince, their beloved Lord. The soldiers began then, under the pyre, to kindle the greatest of funeral fire. Clouds of wood-smoke ascended in billows, black over blaze. The roar of the flames overcame the wails of lamentation. The wind-surge grew still. Beowulf's bone-house the inferno broke, hot unto his heart. Sad of spirit, the soldiers grieved for the sorrow in their souls, the demise of their Lord. And then did an old woman of the Geats, bewailing her woe, her tresses bound up, sing a sorrowful lay. She keened a dirge of unrelenting times of unhappiness to come, countless deaths, the assaults of armies, of shame and bondage. The Heavens swallowed the smoke.

Then did the men of the Geats make a mound upon the headland. It was lofty and imposing, visible far and wide to sea-going sailors voyaging o'er the waves. After the space of ten days their toil had built a monument unto the battle-brave man. They encompassed the remnant of the funeral-pyre with a rampart, the worthiest wall that the most skilled workers could construct. In this barrow did they place the precious booty, rings and gems, treasure that the war-minded men had erstwhile plundered from the hoard. They suffered the Earth to hold the treasure of warriors, consigning gold unto the ground. There does it yet remain, as useless to mortals as it was of yore.

And then, round the mound, rode twelve warriors, bold in battle, sons of Chieftains. They did bemoan their grief, bewail them their King, chant a dirge and tell tales of the man. His valor did they exalt. His deeds of bravery did they acclaim.

It is thus fitting that a man should laud his friend and Liege-Lord with words, and love him in his heart, when he must needs depart forth from his Earthly body.

In this way did the men of the Geats, his hearth-companions, lament the fall of their Lord Beowulf. They said he was, of all the Kings in the world, the most benevolent and most generous of men, the most gracious unto his people, and the most desirous of glory.

...

Postscript

By

John Mitchell Kemble, Esq., M.A.

The introductory canto of the poem Beowulf is devoted to the mythic hero Scyld, the descendant of Sceaf (for the patronymic Scefing does not of itself imply so near a relationship as that of father and son, although it is probable that this was contemplated by the poet). Both Sceaf and Scyld occur in the mythic genealogies of the Saxon Kings, among the remote ancestor of Woden, and it will not be difficult to show that they are the heroes of our poem.

Of Sceaf, it is related that he was cast adrift, as a child, in an ark upon the waters, with a sheaf (Anglo Saxon: sceaf) of corn at his head, whence his name; that the waves bore him upon the coast of Slesvig, and that, being looked upon as a prodigy, and carefully educated, he finally became sovereign of the land.

The Saxon Chronicle, A.D. 854, places at the head of the West Saxon Genealogy, Sceaf, the son of Noah, born in the ark; with this the MS. Genealogy, Cott. MS. Tib. B. 5. Fol. 22, which was written down between A.D. 973 and 975, agrees. In this, I see not only the necessary result of engrafting heathen upon Judaic myths, but also a confused remembrance of the heathen myth itself.

The Langobards, a race in many respects closely connected with the Anglo-Saxons, place Sceafa at the head of their mythic kings, and this is confirmed by the Traveler's Song, which in l.64 gives Sceafa as the king, that is, the first king and founder of the Langobards.

The introductory canto of Beowulf relates that Scyld, a famous and victorious chieftain, grew to this power after having been originally found as an outcast; l.12.13. It proceeds to describe how, after his death, his comrades, by his own command, placed his body in his ship, and so committed it to the winds and the waves. Above the corpse was placed a golden ensign, and the bark was laden with arms and with treasures no less costly than those which they, who in the beginning had sent him alone over the waters, had furnished him with; l. 72, &c. Thus was he suffered to float away into the wide sea, none knew whither.

It is thus clear that the author of Beowulf attributes to Scyld the legend elsewhere and usually given to Sceaf. But that it belongs in reality to Sceaf, and not to Scyld, may fairly be argued from the fact that only this poem attributes it to the latter hero. At the same time, it is not to be overlooked that a MS. Genealogy (MSS. Bibl. Reg. Paris, No. 6055) says of Scyld, *Iste primus inhabitator Germaniae fuit*, probably with reference to this legend. On the contrary, the Danish accounts of the hero, Skjold, Odin's son, and founder of the race of the Skjoldungar, as Scyld is of the Scyldingas, know nothing whatever of Sceaf or of the exposure. As I shall hereafter have occasion to return to Scyld's name, I will only now state my opinion that Sceaf and Scyld may be, in fact, identical. This seems to follow, from the statement of Aethelweard, that Sceaf was landed on Scani (not Scandinavia), compared with the assertion in the Fornmanna Sogur 5, 239, that Skjold was Skanunga godh, as well as from the passage quoted from the Paris MS. I will now only add that Aethelweard and the poem speak of arms and treasures which were laid in the vessel with the sleeping child, omitting all mention of the *sheaf,* which is not only alluded to in the name, but is, as I will hereafter show, essential to the legend.

The introductory canto of the poem then goes on to name Beo the son and successor of Scyld Scefing, and here again we find a remarkable and satisfactory coincidence between the poem and the traditions elsewhere preserved to us. In every one of the genealogies which go as far back as to these mythic princes, we have the same three names Sceaf, Scyld, Beo, and in the same order. Although, therefore, Beo, in the poem, plays a most unimportant part, we may supply from other sources the legends which were current respecting him. As far as we can see, the principal, if not the only, reason for introducing him into the poem, was the wish to connect Hrothgar, the Danish hero of the adventure, with the Angle Scyld. The assertion is therefore made that Hrothgar and his brothers are the sons of Healfdene, the son of Beo the Scylding, an assertion entirely at variance with all tradition. But Beo the Scylding, who is disposed of in about a dozen lines of the introductory and the first canto of the poem, is no such unimportant person in our mythic history. In the library of Trin. Coll. Cambridge, and in the Bibl. Royale at Paris, are two pedigrees on rolls, containing the royal lines of various lands, and, among them, that of England till the reign of Henry VI.

These genealogies are obviously made up of very ancient materials, and from them I take the following line of successions:

MS. Trin. Noah. Japhet. Strepheus. Bedegius. Guala. Hadra. Sternodius. *Sceph. Sceldius. Boerinus.*

MS. Par. Noah. Japhet. Strepheus. Bedegius. Gulla. Hadra. Stermodius. *Steph. Steldlus. Boerinus.*

Now it is obvious that the *t* in the Paris MS. is a mere, and a very common, blunder for *c,* and that we must read *Scef, Sceld,* in both. But, in the third name, there lurks another and similar error. At the time when these MSS. were written down, the English *r* had assumed a peculiar form closely resembling that of the Saxon *w,* which, in these copies made by persons to whom the Saxon letters were no longer intelligible, has been mistaken for it. In both copies, as well as in the MS. Bibl. Publ. Gg. 4, 25, I therefore undoubtingly read Boe-winus. That this is the Beo Scylding of our poem is certain. In the first place, he occupies the position given to that hero in all the genealogies, and, in the next place, the variation between -wine and-wulf in the name is unimportant, and of continual recurrence. To which may be added the fact that *Boerinus* is utterly devoid of meaning in every one of the Teutonic tongues. These two rolls now proceed to furnish us with the following important lists of Beo's sons:

MS. Trin. Cinrincius. Gothus. Jutus. Suethedus. Dacus. Wandalus. Gethus. Fresus. Geatte.

MS. Par. Cininicus. Gothus. Juthus. Suethedus. Dacus. Wandalus. Ghecius. Fresus. Geathus.

Beo the Scylding is then no less a person than the father of the *Eponymi* of all the great Northern tribes. This seems to account for the existence of the introductory canto of the poem itself, which has in fact nothing to do with the rest of the story, and is not included by the scribe in the numbering of the cantos.

That this opens new views respecting not only Beo, but Scyld, Sceaf, and the whole line of their mythic predecessors will readily be seen; these views it is desirable to develop. The name of Beowulf is in itself a difficulty. Scarcely a name can be found in the whole list which has been subjected to so many and such capricious changes, from which I argue that, at a very early period, it was no longer intelligible to the reciters or transcribers. Except in the legends in question, I do not remember ever to have seen it and, if it be the case that it was not borne by men, it furnishes a strong presumption that it was not the name of a *man,* but of a *god,* or at least of such a godlike hero as Saxneat, Woden's son, (the well known and much disputed Saxnot of the Saxon renunciation) or Sigufrit, whom Lachmann has, with striking probability, enrolled among the gods. And even as Sigufrit or Sigurdr, from a god of light and splendor, perhaps another form of Baldur himself, first becomes the hero of the Volsungar, and finally sinks into the merely mortal Siegfried of the Nibelungen legend, so may the old god Beowulf, after passing through the form of the heroic Beo (Beowulf), the Scylding and father of the Northern tribes, have sunk a step further into Beowulf the Waegmunding, the nephew of Hygelac and friend of Hrothgar.

The whole character of this last named warrior's exploits bears a supernatural stamp: he slays Nicors [sea-monsters] by night, l. 838, 1144, for seven whole days he swims against Breca, l. 1028, and, when dragged by the monsters of the deep to the bottom of the abyss, he is there able to contend with and subdue his adversaries, l. 1101, &c. He possesses the strength of thirty men, l. 756; unarmed, and unprovided with defence of any kind, he attacks and slays the fiendish Grendel, l. 1331, &c.; under the waters he slaughters Grendel's mother, and that with a sword forged by the giants in the time of the flood, and such as none but himself could have wielded, l. 3113, &c. 3377, &c.; he engages in battle with the dragon, and vanquishes his opponent, although he must give up his own life in the contest. He is represented throughout as a defender, a protecting and redeeming being.

The main difficulty in this view of the case rests upon the recorded family relations. Beowulf is, in one form, the son of Scyld, the son of Sceaf. In the other, he is the son of Ecgtheow the Waegmunding, and the nephew of Hygelac, but here it strikes one at once with surprise that he is found in this poem alone. He occurs in no Angle or Danish list of kings. He stands alone in the legend, and leaves no children to succeed him on the throne, which, after his death, is possessed by his kinsman Wiglaf.

"For a long while," says the poem itself, "the Angles did not hold him worthy of the throne," l. 4362, [sic] &c., a contradiction utterly inexplicable, seeing that his great exploits were well known in his native land, and which, to me, seems neither more nor less than a reference of the poet himself to the non-appearance of the hero in the legends. These difficulties vanish at once if we look upon him as the heroic and later representative of the godlike Beowulf, and the new family connection with Hrethel's house is caused by the necessity of bringing him into the legend; with Hygelac, he stands in this merely accidental connection, for with the subject of the poem, Hygelac has in reality nothing to do. Nor is this alteration of descents, when a godlike or mythic legend becomes popularized into an epic form, so strange and unexampled. The Nibelungen Lied, for example, which in many cases furnishes most interesting analogies with our own poem, makes the old Niflungar, (even in the Old Norse form confounded with the Burgundian

Gjukingar) not sons of Gibicho (O. Nor. Giuki. A. S. Gifeca. Trav. Song, l. 38.), but of Dankrat.

How far the supposition of Beowulf's identity with the earlier hero of the name may be reconciled with the later legend, which represents him as Ecgtheow's son, must be left to more favorable circumstances, and more learned enquirers to decide; but the divinity of the earlier Beowulf I hold for indisputable. Whether he be a progenitor, a new-birth, of Woden himself, or an independent hero, Woden's descendant by a mortal nymph (and what he is I will presently examine), he is to all intents and purposes a godlike nature, and enquiry may one day teach us that he also had rites and altars among some one of the many tribes of the North. At present, it is enough that we see him placed, as he universally is, among Woden's ancestors, and in the same relation as Geat, Finn and others, who, from being gods, have sunk into epic heroes; that he is the son of Scyld, who is expressly stated to be the god of the Scanungar, and who, according to various accounts, is sometimes a progenitor, sometimes a descendent of Woden, but in the highest mythologic view only a representative of Woden himself; lastly, that he is the father of those mythic heroes who are the *Eponymi* of all the Northern tribes.

That the legends which once belonged to him have long perished away is a misfortune which he shares with a majority of Woden's mythic ancestors. But, even here, we may perhaps at some time or other find ourselves not altogether in the dark. If my conjecture be allowed that the second Beowulf, with his supernatural exploits, is but a shadow of the first, the exploits themselves may be raised from their heroic to a more godlike character, may belong to the god Beowulf, the son of Scyld, to the god Thunor (Thor), the son of the god Woden (Odin), or, in the highest point of view, to the god Woden himself.

I will now attempt to show that these views are capable of support from the nature of the genealogies themselves, a task which I undertake with the more readiness, because it will lead me to some enquiries of considerable interest, and, as I hope, such as to clear up the yet untouched and obscure mythological relations of our earlier heroes. The name of Beowulf is found under the following forms: Beo, Beu, Beau, Beawa, Beowius, Beowinus, Boerinus, Beowulf, Bedwius, Beaf, Beir. It is well known that the simple and the compound name are frequently equivalent. Thus, Hygelac is called Hygd. l. 3849, 4340 [sic]; Finn's father is God-wine or God-wulf; Hroar in Norse (Saxo's Ro, Roe, &c.) is accompanied by a corresponding Hrothgeir, our Hrothgar. In the Hervarar Saga (Fornald. Sog. 1, 490, &c.), one and the same prince is called Hloer or Hlothwer. Grimm says (Deut. Myth.

Stammtaf. xvii), "Wolf is equivalent to Wolfgang, Regin or Regino to Reginhart, Dieto to Dietrich, Liuba to Liebgart: hence also Beowulf and Beowine correspond."

I therefore hold Beo or Beow to be the real form of the name, and consider the three first ways of spelling it to be intended for this only. Beawa is a farther formation of the same kind as Hadra, Sceldwa, and Sceafa, a reading which I prefer to Sceaf. Beowius, which occurs in several MSS., is only Beow, for these MSS. add –ius to almost every name which ends in a consonant. From what has been said, Beowine, Beowulf and Boewine are equivalent to Beow. Beaf and Beir, which occur only in the Fornaldar Sog., may at once be rejected as Norse blunders; Bedwius must be looked to hereafter.

Now, the Old-Saxons, and most likely other conterminal tribes, called their harvest-month (probably part of August and September) by this very name of Beo or Bewod; thus beuuo *segetum.* Helj. 79, 14. Kilian. bouw, *arvum. messis;* in Bavaria, Bau *seges,* bauen *seminare;* bewod, *messis.* Helj. 78, 16. Teutonista. bouwt *messis.* wijnbouwt *vindemia.*

Beo or Beow is therefore in all probability a god of agriculture and fertility, and gives his name to a month, as the goddesses Eostre and Hredhe did to April and March. It strengthens this view of the case that he is the grandson of Sceaf, *manipulus frumenti,* with whom he is perhaps in fact identical. I have already remarked that the note in the Paris roll, which makes Scyld the first inhabitant of Germany, rests upon a confusion of Sceafa and Sceldwa, if indeed these be not, in fact, one and the same person. Sceafa then, in the Angle legend, is the first inhabitant of Germany; that is, Sceafa the god is the origin of everything in Anglia (for Sceafa the god when degraded into a hero is of course received *ab hominibus terrae illius),* while Beowa the god, only another form of Sceafa himself, is the father and founder of all the Germanic races. Nor is it any objection to this hypothesis that Beowa should be the hero of a legend of conquests and struggles, which would be the case were my supposition admitted, that the deeds of Beowulf the Waegmunding are shadows of the deeds of Beowulf the Scylding; for Thunor and Woden are not only gods of battle and victory, but worshipped also as rulers of the weather and granters of the gifts of the earth, of fertility and increase.

It has already been remarked that Sceafa is not necessarily Beowulf's grandfather. Some lists, on the contrary, place him at the very head of the genealogy and give several names between him and Sceldwa. He is then omitted before Sceldwa and takes the place of Strepheus.

It would be an agreeable occupation to pursue these speculations through other genealogies, but I feel that this would lead me into a disquisition not suited to the immediate objects of this preface, or to my present limits, and I therefore will reserve these enquiries, as well as a complete examination of the Traveler's Song, for a work expressly devoted to the heathen mythology of England. I now return to matters more closely connected with the poem of Beowulf. Sceafa, Sceldwa, and Beowa have been shown to be gods, but they appear no longer as gods in the poem—they are heroes, and heroes of Anglia. Of these, Scyld alone is known to the Danes, and he is the founder of their Skjoldungar, as Scyld is the founder of the Anglo-Saxon Scyldingas. Now the chroniclers of the Saxons expressly claim Sceaf, whose place Scyld occupies in the poem, for Anglia. Malmesbury and Simeon of Durham place the landing of the infant Sceaf in Slesvig, which was then called Haitheby, and both these writers, as well as the chronicler, MS. Gg. 4, 25, say that the land was Vetus Anglia, whence the Angles came to Britain, and further define it as situated between *Gothos* (read *Juthos,* the Jutes in Jutland) and *Saxones,* the inhabitants of Nordalbingia.

This testimony would be quite decisive even if it stood alone, but this it does not. Hygelac, Beowulf's uncle, reigns in the territory which had been ruled by Offa, and that Offa belongs to Angle, and not to Danish tradition, it must now be my aim to show. In the Langfedgatal and Saxo we have, no doubt, Varmundr, Wermundus, Uffi, Huhlekr, &c. The Langfedgatal, which is the oldest and most complete of the Norse genealogies, is however by no means the authority. On examination, it is found to consist of three distinct portions, the first of which contains many names from the Biblical history, several from classical sources, and a tolerably complete Anglo-Saxon genealogy, all of which it attempts to connect with gods or heroes of Scandinavia; the second portion, on the contrary, gives a real Norse genealogy from Odin to Haraldr Harfagri, and this, which alone is followed by Snorro in the Heimskringla, knows nothing whatever of the heroes of Beowulf, unless the enumeration of Athils among the kings of Sweden, and a hint respecting Ingialldr and Swipdagr are to be considered as approaches to the cycle of our legends; the third portion contains the usual Norse genealogy, including Wermundr, but says not a word of Uffi, &c. To Saxo, and his laudable anxiety to connect in one work, for the honor of his fatherland, all the legends which he found here and there current respecting any princes of the Teutonic stock, we probably owe the appearance of Wermundr, Uffi, &c. like the Jutish Hamlet and the mythic Horwendil in the legends of Denmark.

Offa's relation to Hygelac is not very clearly made out. The last-named prince is a son of Hrethel, a name which to the best of my knowledge occurs only in this poem. He succeeds his elder brother on the throne, but Offa's wife lives in his palace and presides there over the feast, and the drinking-bouts of the earls, and this office could only belong to a lady nearly related to the prince. Now this lady is herself a mystic personage enough. It is related of her that she was no mild distributor of treasures, but on the contrary a fierce virago who engaged in battles with warriors. But, the poet adds, as a variation of the story (other Saegdon, l. 3887, &c.) that being, by the advice of her father Haereth, given in marriage to Offa, she left off her violent practices and, accordingly, she appears in Hygelac's court exercising the peaceful duties of a princess. Now this whole representation can hardly be other than the modern, altered, and Christian view of a Valkyrie or swan-maiden, and, almost in the same words, the Nibelungen Lied relates of Brunnhilde, the flashing shield-maid of the Edda, that, with her virginity, she lost her mighty strength and warlike habits.

There are other Angles who appear in the poem of Beowulf, whose names it is now almost impossible to find in any other Northern legend. Their relation to the heroes of the poem and their deeds are alike lost to us. Hygelac is thus called Swertling's nephew (l. 2406), but who Swert-ing, *the son of darkness,* (A.S. sweart) is, I cannot say. At the same time, I observe that Swearta occurs in the genealogy of Deira, therefore also Angle, and that some authorities for Swearta give Swerting.

The successor of Beowulf on the throne of Anglia is, in our poem, Wiglaf, the son of Wihstan or Weohstan, and one of the Waegmunding family. The usual law in A. S. family names renders it probable that the *i* in Wiglaf is short, as in Wihstan; that is, that the name is compounded , not with wig *bellum,* but wih *templum,* and the O. Sax. form of the name would therefore be Wiglef or Wihlef. According to my view, this prince is the Wiglec, Wiglet of the Norse genealogies who is given as Garmund's *predecessor.* But the name itself is not Norse (laf in A. S., lef in Old Saxon are O. Nor. leifr), and a good reason may be given for the alteration in the order of the succession. Many of the Norse legends know nothing of Wiglet, Garmund's predecessor, and this arises partly from the necessity of connecting this latter prince with Frothi or some other Danish hero. The author of Beowulf, however, had his own reasons for putting Wiglaf after Beowulf. In the first place, the introduction of Beowulf himself disturbed the natural order of the succession, and, in the next, the poet who looked upon Garmund as Offa's uncle (nefa Garmundes, l. 3919), and not his father, probably considered Hemming as this famous prince's father and predecessor, vid. l. 3885, 3918, where he is called Hemminges maeg, and where I read maeg *filius,* not maeg *affinis.*

Having thus, to the best of my power, cleared up the Angle legends which occur in Beowulf, it is desirable to bestow a few words upon the other races and such of their traditions as have become mingled with our own; the principal of these are the Danish and Frisian legends. In order to connect his Danish heroes with Beowulf and Hygelac, and probably remembering that Hrothgar and his brothers were Skjoldungar, the poet asserts their father, Healfdene, to be a son of Beo the Scylding. This is obviously at variance with all tradition. Hrothgar and Halga, it was asserted in the preface, are the Hroar and Helgi of the North. In calling them sons of Healfdene our poem is then right, as the Konungs Hrolfs Kraka saga relates (Fornald. Sog. i. 3, &c.). But, in this account, we hear nothing of Heorogar, Hrothgar's elder brother, Halga til (the good) answers but little to the Helgi of the Northmen, and Signy (not Elan), their sister, is married to Earl Saevil, while our poem says nothing whatever of her husband, further than that he was a Scylfing, a race connected with the Scyldings on one hand, and with the Niflings on the other, and who appear to reign in Sweden, since Ongentheow is called Gomela Scylfing. Hrothwulf, Hrothgar's cousin (suhtor-faedera), in our poem probably Halga's son, was also asserted to be the Hrolfr of the Northmen.

But, with these names, the resemblance between the legends ends, and we have no cause to believe that the Norse story of these princes was known to the author of our poem. On the other hand, the Anglo-Saxon account contains circumstances not known to the Northmen. From these two facts, it may fairly be concluded that the Anglo-Saxon legends are not borrowed from the Norse, but far rather national traditions which had grown up in Anglia, but whose subjects naturally enough were kings of a neighboring island, standing in relations of friendship or hostility to the Angles themselves.

It is worthwhile to cast our eyes for a few moments upon the Norse accounts themselves. The names of Hroar and Helgi occur in no less than ten genealogical lists, Chronicles, &c. in the first vol. of Langebek's Scriptores, in Saxo Grammaticus, and in a Saga expressly devoted to Hrolf Kraki. But here we see, without much surprise, that the Northern accounts themselves are, in the highest degree, inconsistent, contradictory, and we may venture to say, in nine cases out of ten, incorrect. The story, as in the Hrolfs Kraka saga, is that Frothi and Halfdan were brothers, that the latter was murdered by his ambitious kinsman, and revenged by his sons Hroar and Helgi. Now, though all the genealogies, &c., give us the line Frothi, Halfdan, Ro, and

Helgi, most of them consider Halfdan as Frothi's son. The list of kings, Langeb. i. 31, attributes Frothi's crime to Halfdan; with this Sven Aggonis (p. 44), Petrus Olai (p. 79), and the so-called chronicle of Eric (p. 151), agree.

The Hrolfr of the various Norse genealogies, and of the Saga, is Helgi's son, and Hroar's nephew. In Beowulf, Hrothulf is equally Hrothgar's nephew, and probably Halga's son. In the few passages of Beowulf and the Traveler's Song where he occurs, there is no allusion to the awful legends of his birth, &c. All that surprises one is that his father Halga is hardly mentioned, and that he shares Hrothgar's kingdom. On the contrary, the Norse legend of Hrolfr is one of strange and mythic nature, and can hardly be reconciled with the genealogies, &c. given in the XIIIth and following centuries, although a portion of it appears to have been known to Snorro (Heimskr. Yngl. Saga. XXXIII. fol. ed. i. 41). The legend of Ingeld who, in Saxo Grammaticus, is represented as luxurious and degenerate until roused into action by the remonstrances of the famous Starcadher (one of the most thoroughly mythic persons in the whole range of Norse traditions), is known to the author of our poem, who, however, never names Starcadher, and considers Ingeld as Froda's son. To him, Hrothgar gives his daughter as a wife, with a view to appease the ancient feud, unsuccessfully, however, as our poem relates. He occurs in nearly all the genealogies, but, in very few of them is he brought in contact with the heroes whom our poet makes his contemporaries, viz. Hrothgar (his nephew), and Hygelac (Swerting's nephew). On the contrary, he is placed in the succession long after the last named prince, but a Frothi is always given as his father (Langeb. i. 15, 19, 21, 28, 31, 47, 85, 153).

Several of these passages give the legend of Ingeld's degeneracy and Starcadher's revenge upon the sons of Swerting, but, according to the object kept in view by each particular writer, Ingeld is sometimes king of Sweden, sometimes of Denmark, &c. &c. The difficulty of reconciling two stories, viz. the death of Frothi by the hands of Hroar and Helgi, and the slaughter of Frothi by the sons of Swerting, has probably created another Frothi here, and caused him to be placed with Ingeld at a period so late in comparison with Hroar. But the Langfedgatal so far rectifies this error as to make Ingeld Halfdan's brother, though it calls them both sons, and not brothers, of Frothi. An Ingeld is one of the heroes of Snorro; he is made by him nearly contemporary with Athils and Helgi. This corresponds tolerably well with our poem, but what seems to identify this prince with our Ingeld is a reference, somewhat obscure indeed, to the degeneracy and weakness which are dispelled by Starcadher's remonstrances.

According to the Heimskringla, i. 46, Ingialldr was one day at play
with Alfr, King Ingvar's son. As the latter proved himself the stronger,
Ingialldr could hardly refrain from tears. His foster-father, Swipdagr, (a
person quite as mythic as, and perhaps no other than, Starcadher), observing
this, adopted means to encourage his pupil. That is, the next day, Swipdagr
caused them to take a wolf's heart and roast it on a skewer, and then he gave
it to Ingialldr, the king's son, to eat. And, thenceforward, was he the most
savage of men and the most ferocious.

But, although Helgi, Hrolfr, Ingialldr, Athils and Halfdan are known
to Snorro, Hroar is not, which, compared with the fact that Saxo, Snorro's
contemporary, is well acquainted with all the details of Hroar's history, leads
to the conclusion that all these legends, though more or less common
property, were extremely varied by different tribes, according to whether the
princes could be more or less closely connected with their own lists of royal
or heroic ancestors. Snorro knows nothing of Hroar, consequently nothing of
the building of Roskeldia (Heorot) which is related in Saxo. From Saxo it
probably was borrowed by the genealogies, &c. (Langeb. i. 31, 79, 131), but
the Anglo-Saxo account confirms it as part of Hroar's legend. Without
entering upon the question what precise part of Scandinavia Hroar and Helgi
belong to, a question which it will never be easy to answer, we may, I think,
fearlessly assert that these two princes, their father Halfdan, their uncles
Frothi and Ingialldr, and Helgi's son Hrolfr, really belong to the Norse cycle
of legends. But they belonged to the Angle cycle too, and this last named
people exercised the right possessed by all peoples, of varying, extending or
contracting the epic material of their traditions. Hence, the Angle traditions
differ in some respects from the Norse and, in this very difference, they
assert their independent origin and independent development.

Although I will not raise Hrothgar and his brothers to the rank of
gods, as I have Beowulf, Geat and Finn, yet I must observe that any attempt
to assign historical dates to these or almost any other princes before the
introduction of Christianity, and with Christianity, leads to nothing but
confusion. All that part of my preface which assigns dates to one prince or to
another, to Beowulf, or to Sigufrit, or which attempts to draw any
conclusions from dates so assigned, I declare to be null and void, upon
whatsoever authority those dates may pretend to rest. The uncritical spirit of
the period to which we owe all the connected accounts of the Northern
heroes has caused the utmost confusion in every branch of legendary and
traditional history, and rendered it almost impossible to separate what has
been unskillfully (luckily for us most unskillfully) patched together, and
which has been formed into a whole only by painful sacrifices of individual

parts. But it is our duty, as far as possible, to remedy this evil by pointing out the seams in the patchwork, by separating the individual portions from the mass, and restoring to them, as well as we can, the integrity of their ancient form. Least of all does it become us to proceed upon the same narrow and confined plan as our forerunners and to repeat, in the nineteenth century, the uncritical blunders of the twelfth century.

But there is great difficulty in the matter and caution is very necessary, lest, in our zeal for system and simplicity, we be led to sacrifice any of that variety which is essential to epic tradition. When we meet with half a dozen repetitions of Odin's name, we know how to deal with them. But the case is not so easy when we have as many Halfdans, Erics, or Frothis, because, in the latter case, there may have been two or more of the same name, and the deeds which belonged to the legend of one hero may have been worked up into the legend of another. In the Norse genealogy, for example, we have several repetitions of Halfdan and Frothi, some of which can fortunately be shown to have arisen out of accidental and foreign variations of a legend which belonged only to one; and this multiplication of descents, generally caused by the necessity of making out a chronological unity, in cases where time is not to be thought of at all, has not only monstrously swelled the lists of kings, but very materially interfered with the just relations of the heroes, for to say successions of the heroes is almost, at once, to assert a false proposition.

In these legends, the whole dramatis personae stand side by side— they do not follow one another. If, in cases of this kind, one could talk of a Frothi I and Frothi II, I should say that Hroar and Helgi belong to the group of the first Frothi, in the various genealogies. That other legends and other heroes belonged also to another group, of which the first Frothi was the centre, was sufficient reason for the existence of a second Frothi. The genealogies are like the catalogue of a mighty sculpture-hall, in which the twelve labours of Hercules shall have been placed in marble groups. The first represents him strangling the serpents, another dashing out the brains of the Erymanthine boar, a third stifling Antaeus, a fourth easing the shoulders of Atlas. On the pedestals of the groups stand the numbers I to XII. Then comes the catalogue-maker and, beginning at the beginning and ending with the end, gives us a succession of twelve heroes of the name of Hercules, with a history of their individual exploits, and, if he be only a little of a pedant too, can tell us to a mile and a month where and when they reigned or laboured. The case is indeed not always so simple, but the process is eternally the same, even because the human understanding works eternally by the same laws and with the same method. Let us turn our eyes for a moment to the third portion of the Langfedgatal, the first two divisions of which I have noticed already. This third portion contains, with unimportant variations, the usual Norse genealogy starting from Odin.

Now here are seven and twenty distinct names of kings, of which a full third may unhesitatingly be expunged. Let Odin remain at the head of the genealogy. Skioldr and Fridleifr, two names of gods already known to us in the Saxon Scyld and Freotholaf, may also remain. But we have two more Fridleifrs, in each case sons of Frode the peaceful, and here each of the Fridleifrs, as well as the second Frode must "make room for honest men." Wermundr has nothing to do with Denmark. Olafr and Danr are sometimes one and the same person, sometimes only different names for Uffi, who belongs as little to Denmark as Wermundr did. In fact, it is by no means clear to me that at least two sets of legends are not mixed up by juxtaposition, in what I have allowed to stand, for I find Danr a great stumbling-block. But this enquiry I leave to the philologists of Denmark.

The Frisians who appear in Beowulf are likewise of considerable interest, from the relation in which they stand to older and godlike heroes, if not gods themselves. Their country is called Fresna-land, l. 5826, Fres-lond, l. 4709, Fres-wael, l. 2133. The people themselves are Fresan, l. 2180, Frysan, l. 5819, Eotenas, l. 2137, 2169, 2275, 2283. Their king is Finn, l. 2155, 2186. Folcwaldan Sunu, l. 2172. He is given as son of Folcwalda and king of the Frisians in the Trav. S. l. 53, but does not appear in the battle of Finnesburh; which city, as well as the yet subsisting borough of Finsbury in London, records his name. But Finn is mythic. Like Sceafa, Beowa and Geat, he and his father Folcwalda appear as Woden's ancestors, and I have already shown that, after all, both he and his father may be no other than Woden himself.

But, like Beowa, he has ceased to be a god and both he and his legend, broken down from the godlike into the heroic, have become material for the epic, and perhaps thus alone has he been rescued from the fate which befell Woden, namely to be degraded from a god of victory, fruitfulness and splendor, into a giant, a sorcerer, or a devil. With Finn the god I have already dealt and have now only to notice him as Finn, the hero and king of Friesland. In the episode of our poem in which he is introduced, he is represented as falling in war against the Danes, who, successively, under Hengest, Oslaf and Guthlaf, fall upon and conquer him. Now it is very clear that none of these are Danish names, any more than Hnaef the Hocing (Bat. Finsb. l. 80. Trav. S. l. 57), who, in l. 2131, is called Healfdene's hero and, in the following line, a Scylding. Although the A.S. poet would no doubt translate the foreign names, as he did by Hroar, Helgi, and the like, yet on other accounts I believe that there is confusion in these legends also, for Hengest, who cannot have been a Dane, is a Frisian hero, appears as such in the genealogy of the kings of Kent, and is the fabled conqueror of Britain. The Hocings, it is also probable, were a Frisian tribe.

The legend, as it stands in Beowulf, when compared with the battle of Finnesburh, is that Hnaef, assisted by Hengest, Ordlaf (Oslaf), Guthlaf, and other heroes, attacks the city of Finn, but falls in the contest. Finn is, however, defeated and deprived of half his kingdom, which appears to be occupied by Hengest's Danes and by the Hocings. And, if, as I believe, Hildeburh is Finn's queen, and a different person from Hoce's daughter, Hnaef's mother, he loses a son also, who is sacrificed upon Hnaef's funeral pile. Hengest, remaining among the Frisians, is, in the following year, set upon and slain by Finn, who being in consequence attacked by the Danes under Guthlaf and Oslaf (Ordlaf, Bat. Finsb. 1. 32), loses his life and crown in the contest. Such is the heroic legend, and one obviously of later growth, but that from which it sprang exists for us no longer. The other Frisians, incidentally mentioned, are of no particular interest. The story of Heremod, alluded to by Hrothgar, is quite lost, and the valuable hints respecting the Waelsing Sigmund (Volsungar, Sigmundr) must be treated of elsewhere.

From the preceding enquiries, it appears to me that I have gained the following results: first, I have vindicated the legends for Anglia, and, next, I have assigned their proper place to the Angle legends, among the traditions of the Teutons. The pointing out the mythological relations of the names which occur in our genealogies may perhaps also be looked upon as an object justifying the pains and space devoted to it. If it does nothing else, it at least shows the principle upon which we must proceed if we wish to have anything like a clear view of what these genealogies meant to convey.

Trinity College Cambridge
Cambridge, England
1835

Glossary of Proper Names

Abel. Son of Adam and Eve, slain by his brother Cain.

Aelfhere. A kinsman of Wiglaf.

Aeschere. Confidant and friend of King Hrothgar. Elder brother of Yrmenlaf. Killed by Grendel's mother, who leaves his head for Beowulf and his followers to find.

Beanstan. Father of Breca. A Bronding.

Beo. Son of Scyld, founder of the dynasty of Scyldings. Father of Healfdene and grandfather of Hrothgar.

Beowulf. Hero of the poem. Son of Ecgtheow, the Geat. Raised by his maternal grandfather Hrethel, King of the Geats. Devoted liegeman of his uncle, King Hygelac. Has the strength of thirty men. Engages in a swimming match with Breca. Aids Hrothgar in his fight against Grendel. Kills Grendel and Grendel's mother. Later becomes king of the Geats. In his old age, fights the Fire-Dragon and kills it, but is slain by the Dragon. Is buried with great honors.

Breca. Beowulf's opponent in the swimming match. Son of Beanstan. A Bronding.

Brondings. A tribe ruled by Breca.

Brosings. A race of dwarfs, who made a famous necklace for the Goddess Freya, which Hama stole from King Eormenric.

Brosinga Mene. The famous necklace made by the Brosings for the Goddess Freya.

Cain. Son of Adam and Eve. Murderer of his brother Abel. Progenitor of Grendel and other monsters.

Daeghrefn. A warrior of the Franks. Killer of Hygelac. Slain by Beowulf in that battle.

Danes. Subjects of Scyld and his descendants. Often called Scyldings.

Eadgils. Swedish prince. Son of Ohthere and brother of Eanmund. Beowulf assists him in taking the crown from his uncle Onela, whom Eadgils slays.

Eanmund. Swedish Prince. Son of Ohthere and brother of Eadgils. Slain by his uncle Onela, together with Heardred, King of the Geats.

Ecglaf. Father of Unferth, who taunts Beowulf.

Ecgtheow. Father of Beowulf. A renowned Waegmunding warrior. Marries daughter of King Hrethel. After killing Heatholaf, a Wylfing, in a feud, he flees his country Geatland and seeks asylum with Hrothgar. Hrothgar pays blood-money to settle the feud.

Ecgwela. A king of the Danes before Scyld. Ancestor of Heremod, the evil king.

Eofor. A hero of the Geats who kills the Swedish King Ongentheow in battle and is rewarded by Hygelac by marriage to his only daughter.

Eomer. Son of Offa and Thryth, king and queen of the Angles.

Eormenric. A king of the Goths, from whom Hama stole the famous necklace, Brosinga Mene.

Finn. King of the Frisians. Husband of Hildeburh, sister to Hnaef, the Danish king. Finn slays Hnaef at Finnesburh. Finn is then murdered by Hnaef's thane Hengest.

Fitela. Son (and nephew) of Sigemund, the Dragon-Slayer.

Folcwalda. Father of Finn, king of the Frisians.

Franks. A Germanic people from the Rhine region. They conquered Gaul about 500 A.D. and killed King Hygelac about 521 A.D.

Freawaru. Danish princess. Daughter of King Hrothgar. Betrothed to Ingeld, the Heathobard prince, in a vain attempt to heal the bloody feud between the Danes and the Heathobards.

Frisians. A Germanic people residing in what is now the Netherlands.

Froda. King of the Heathobards and father of Ingeld. Killed in the Danish-Heathobard feud.

Garmund. Father of Offa, king of the Angles.

Geats. Tribe which dwelt in Southern Sweden. Ruled by Hrethel, Haethcyn, Hygelac, Heardred and Beowulf. The Swedes were their mortal enemies. There is scant record of the Geats in accounts after the age of Beowulf, and no one knows what became of them.

Grendel. A man-eating monster. Descendant of the spawn of Cain, who dwells in the fens and moors. He ravages the Danes for twelve years. He is overcome by Beowulf, and dies of his wound. His arm and hand are hung high in Heorot, Hrothgar's hall. Grendel's head is cut off by Beowulf, who presents it to Hrothgar as a trophy.

Guthlaf. A Danish warrior. Follower of Hnaef and Hengest. When his brother Hunlaf is slain, he presses Hengest to assault Finn.

Haereth. Father of Hygelac's Queen Hygd.

Haethcyn. Son of Hrethel and brother of Hygelac. Kills his brother Herebeald by accident. Becomes king of the Geats after his father Hrethel dies of grief. Is slain by the Swedes at Ravenswood, fighting against Ongentheow.

Halga. Surnamed the Good. Danish prince. Younger brother of Hrothgar. Father of Hrothulf.

Hama. Steals the famous necklace, Brosinga Mene, from the Gothic King Eormenric.

Healfdene. Grandson of Scyld and son of Beo. Danish king. Father of Heorogar, Halga, Hrothgar and Yrse, who married Onela, king of the Swedes.

Heardred. Son of Hygelac and Hygd, king and queen of the Geats. Becomes, as a youth, king of the Geats upon his father's death, with Beowulf acting in the capacity of Regent. Killed in battle by the Swedish King Onela, whereupon Beowulf becomes king of the Geats.

Heathobards. A Germanic tribe, of which Froda is king. After Froda is killed in battle with the Danes, his son Ingeld succeeds him. Hrothgar marries his daughter Freawaru to Ingeld in a futile attempt to heal the feud between the Heathobards and the Danes, but, in the end, Heorot is destroyed as a result of the enmity between the tribes.

Heatholaf. A Wylfing warrior slain by Beowulf's father, Ecgtheow. Hrothgar pays blood-money to settle the feud after Ecgtheow is exiled.

Helmings. The tribe to which Hrothgar's Queen Wealhtheow belonged.

Hemming. Kinsman of the Angle King Offa.

Hengest. Danish king. Succeeds Hnaef, who is killed by Finn, the Frisian king. Hengest later gets vengeance by slaying Finn.

Heorogar. Danish king. Elder brother of Hrothgar. Son of Healfdene and father of Heoroweard.

Heorot. The mighty mead-hall built by King Hrothgar. It is attacked by Grendel for twelve years. Beowulf mortally wounds Grendel in Heorot. It is so named for the hart (or stag) antlers which adorn it. Finally consumed by flames in the fatal feud between the Heathobards and the Danes.

Heoroweard. Son of Heorogar.

Herebeald. Eldest son of Hrethel, king of the Geats, and brother of Hygelac. Accidentally killed by his brother Haethcyn when his arrow goes astray.

Heremod. An earlier king of the Danes. He demonstrated great promise because of his military victories, but his reign was a time of great sorrow on account of his cruel and avaricious nature. He seeks sanctuary from the Jutes, who subsequently slay him.

Hereric. Uncle of Heardred and brother of Queen Hygd.

Hildeburh. Wife of Finn, daughter of Danish King Hoc, and sister of Hnaef.

Hnaef. King of the Danes. Killed by Finn in the battle of Finnesburh.

Hoc. King of the Danes. Father of Hildeburh and Hnaef.

Hondscio. One of the fourteen Geat warriors who accompany Beowulf to Heorot. He is killed by Grendel before Beowulf tears off the monster's arm.

Hrethel. King of the Geats. Father of Hygelac and grandfather of Beowulf.

Hrethric. Son of Hrothgar and Wealhtheow.

Hrothgar. Danish king who builds Heorot. Married to Wealhtheow. Beloved liege lord and generous giver of gifts. Son of Healfdene. Beset by Grendel's assaults. Aided by Beowulf in return for Hrothgar's assistance to Beowulf's father.

Hrothmund. Son of Hrothgar and Wealhtheow.

Hrothulf. Son of Halga and Yrse. Nephew of Hrothgar. He becomes king of the Danes when he kills Hrothgar's son Hrethric, and is himself slain by Heorogar's son Heoroweard.

Hrunting. Famous ancient sword of Unferth, which he lends to Beowulf. The weapon is of little avail against Grendel's mother.

Hygd. Queen of the Geats. Wife of Hygelac and daughter of Haereth. Mother of Heardred. Beowulf gives her the necklace bestowed upon him by Wealhtheow. After the death of Hygelac, she offers the crown to Beowulf, but he refuses it.

Hygelac. King of the Geats. Uncle and liege lord of Beowulf. Son of Hrethel. Dies in a battle against the Franks on the Rhine about 521 A.D.

Ingeld. King of the Heathobards. Son of Froda. Hrothgar offers his daughter Freawaru in marriage to Ingeld in order to reconcile the feud, but this proves to be of no avail.

Jutes. Another name for Finn's tribe, the Frisians.

Naegling. Renowned sword of Beowulf.

Offa. King of the Angles and son of Garmund. Father of Eomer. Married to the evil Queen Thryth, who is contrasted with the good Queen Hygd.

Ohthere. Swedish king. Son of Ongentheow. Father of Eanmund and Eadgils. Brother of Onela.

Onela. Swedish king. Married to Yrse, Hrothgar's sister. Assumes the throne upon Ohthere's death. Killed by his nephew Eadgils, Ohthere's son, who then takes the crown.

Ongentheow. King of Sweden. Father of Ohthere and Onela. Kills Haethcyn, king of the Geats, at the battle of Ravenswood and is subsequently slain by the Geat warrior Eofor in the ensuing conflict.

Oslaf. Danish warrior. Thane of Hnaef and Hengest.

Ravenswood. Forest where the battle takes place between Swedes and Geats when Haethcyn and Ongentheow are killed.

Scefing. Applied to Scyld, and meaning "son of Scef."

Scyld. Founder of the Danish dynasty of this epic. Father of Beo, grandfather of Healfdene, and great-grandfather of Hrothgar. After his death, his body is placed in a boat and set adrift. This is a fitting counterpoint to his appearance in Dane-land as a baby set adrift in a boat.

Sigemund. Famous dragon-killer. Son of Waels. Uncle (and father) of Fitela.

Swerting. King of the Geats. Grandfather of Hygelac and father of Hrethel.

Thryth. Wife of Offa, king of the Angles. Of a vicious and unwomanly disposition, later tamed.

Unferth. Son of Ecglaf. Killed his brother. A thane of Hrothgar. Taunts Beowulf for having undertaken the swimming match with Breca. Lends Beowulf his sword, Hrunting, for the fight against Grendel's mother.

Waegmundings. Geat family to which Beowulf, Wihstan and Wiglaf belong.

Waels. Father of Sigemund.

Wealhtheow. Danish queen. Wife of Hrothgar. Mother of Hrethric and Hrothmund. Gracious and courtly. Fearful for the welfare of her young sons after her husband's demise.

Weland. A renowned metal-smith, famous for the quality of his workmanship. He crafted the chain-mail shirt Beowulf inherits from his grandfather, Hrethel.

Wendels. Vandals. Tribe of Wulfgar, King Hrothgar's herald and retainer.

Weohstan. A Waegmunding and father of Wiglaf. Killer of Eanmund.

Wiglaf. Son of Weohstan and relative of Beowulf. Only warrior to remain faithful to Beowulf in the final battle with the Dragon. He becomes king of the Geats after the death of Beowulf.

Wonred. A Geat. Father of Wulf and Eofor.

Wulf. Geat warrior. Fights Swedish King Ongentheow at Ravenswood, where Ongentheow wounds him in hand-to-hand combat, whereupon his brother Eofor kills Ongentheow.

Wulfgar. A Vandal prince, who serves Hrothgar as his herald.

Wylfings. A Germanic tribe whose members included Heatholaf, who was slain by Ecgtheow, Beowulf's father.

Yrmenlaf. A Danish warrior. Younger brother of Aeschere.

Yrse. Daughter of Healfdene. Wife of Swedish King Onela.

Beowulf 102

Genealogies

THE GEATS

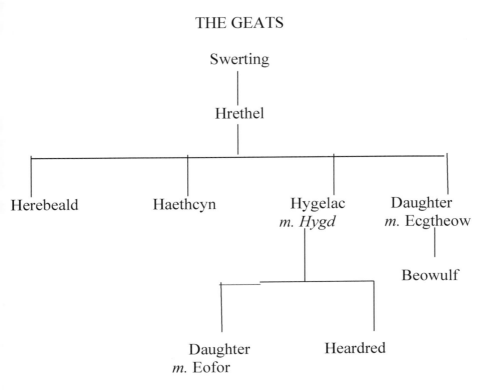

THE SWEDES

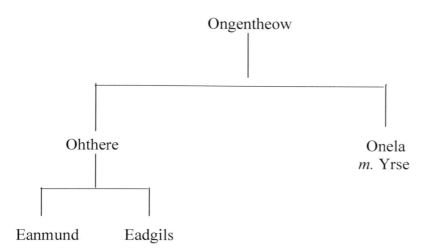

THE DANES

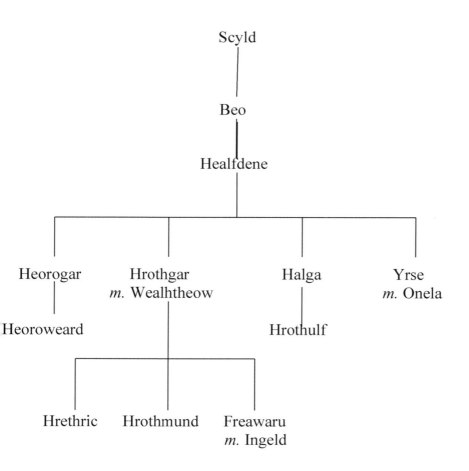

The End

...

Made in United States
Orlando, FL
19 April 2022

16988380R00061